PRAISE FOR *FREE TO BE ME*

"Free To Be Me is more than a memoir—it's a sacred transmission of healing, truth, and fierce feminine power. Elicia Woodford writes with breathtaking honesty, beauty, and depth. Her words don't just move you; they change you. This book is a heart-opening, soul-stirring companion for anyone walking the spiral path of freedom and homecoming. I'll be recommending it again and again to every seeker ready to reclaim their wholeness."

~**Eva Andrea**, Author, Mystic, & Writing Mentor

"This book is a luminous act of truth-telling and transformation—a map and a mirror for anyone ready to reclaim their authentic self.

With every page, Elicia invites us into her most tender, powerful, and raw moments, guiding us through her empowered journey of healing from the inside out—arriving at a place of true love and liberation. With fierce honesty, emboldened clarity, and disarming humor, she unpacks the emotional wounds and toxic patterns that once shaped her life and reveals how she alchemized them into wisdom, purpose, and vibrant wholeness.

As a Transformation Guide, I was deeply moved and inspired by her unwavering commitment to the inner work—to break cycles, reclaim her health, and unleash her truth. Her feminine courage is uplifting. Her soulful wildness, elevating. And her journey, nothing short of inspiring.

Reading this memoir feels like sitting in a sacred circle with a trusted friend.

Elicia doesn't just write her story—she *owns* it, with a voice that is fierce, unflinching, and utterly human. This is a memoir for every woman who's ever doubted her strength and needs a reminder that our scars are sacred. A stunning debut that left me in awe."

~**Shereen H. Eltobgy (SHE),** Master Flow Coach & Creator of the Radiance Alchemy Path™

"I read *Free to Be Me* in one day; I couldn't put it down. I was immediately captured by the raw vulnerability and authenticity of her writing. I was able to walk her journey with her, and her acceptance of herself allowed me to embrace parts of myself I had struggled with. It's a beautiful and very worthwhile read."

~**Christopher Goodsell**, CEO

"*Free to Be Me* is a captivating memoir highlighting the incredible journey of Elicia Woodford as she courageously makes her way down the sometimes heartbreaking, sometimes glorious path to evolve, heal, serve, and love at greater levels.

Elicia's pilgrimage through various countries and relationships—be it lovers, friends, or her beloved canine companions–keeps you turning the pages and wanting more. As she bravely walks her talk to dismantle the patterns of her childhood emotional wounds to reveal her truest self, she simultaneously embarks on a spiritual journey that evokes unexpected gifts and transformation. Whether Elicia is dancing with life or running from it, she repeatedly returns to the inner longing of her soul to embody all aspects of herself to feel at home in her own heart."

~**Tammy Billups**, Certified Interface Therapist, International Holistic Healer, and Award Winning Author of four books, including *Animal Soul Contracts*

"The raw truth and honesty of Elicia's empowering journey to the depths and heights of life's expression so illustrates the presence of all three water signs in her astrological chart. Elicia's willingness to take the outer journey to places around the world, and her inner journey into the depths of hell and the heights of heaven, speaks to her astrological wiring. In *Free To Be Me*, Elicia has birthed her 'baby' in perfect Divine timing."

~**Lorelei Robbins**, Astrologer, Joy Guru

FREE
TO BE ME

A MEMOIR OF TRAUMA, HEALING, AND REBIRTH

ELICIA WOODFORD

Free To Be Me
A Memoir of Trauma, Healing, and Rebirth

Copyright © 2025. Elicia Woodford.

All rights reserved. No part of this publication may be reproduced, distributed, or transmitted in any form or by any means, including photocopying, recording, or other electronic or mechanical methods, without the prior written permission of the copyright holder, except in the case of brief quotations embodied in critical reviews and certain other noncommercial uses permitted by copyright law.

ISBN: 979-8-9928630-8-6

Book Design: Transcendent Publishing
Book Cover: Lucinda Rae
Editor: Mary Rembert
Photographer (Aix-en-Provence, France): Julie Mannina
Makeup (Aix-en-Provence, France): Claire Hameury

Author's Note:

This book is a deeply personal journey of transformation and faith. I have done my best to capture the truth of my experiences with honesty and heart. To respect the privacy of certain individuals, some names and identifying details have been changed. However, the essence of each story remains true to the spirit of what was lived and learned.

Printed in the United States of America.

DEDICATION

To my inner child, and all of your inner children

TABLE OF CONTENTS

Preface xiii
Bad Bunny 1
Million-Dollar Diamond 17
Two Worlds 29
Fasting and Excretion .33
Portal Horse 47
Birthday Wish 67
Frog Call 79
Sun Dial 89
Hummingbird 95
Spirit Babies 109
Mother's Milk 115
The Seed 123
Girl Girl 129
Gypsy Carnival 137
Disney Movie 143

Wisdom's Tears 153
Toxic Hope 159
Shaking the Tree 165
Cosmic Game Show 173
Feminine Filter 181
Drops of God 191
Eclipse Portal 199
The Scent of Roses 207
Epilogue 213
Acknowledgments 215
About the Author 217
Bonus Gift 219

"The truth about our childhood is stored up in our body, and although we can repress it, we can never alter it. Our intellect can be deceived, our feelings manipulated, and conceptions confused, and our body tricked with medication. But someday our body will present its bill, for it is as incorruptible as a child, who, still whole in spirit, will accept no compromises or excuses, and it will not stop tormenting us until we stop evading the truth."

—Alice Miller

PREFACE

I told myself I was just having fun, but that was a lie. The truth? I would have done anything for Nic's love. I ignored my higher self because, unconsciously, my wounded inner child desired to be loved by Nic.

I swore I would never be with him again. I knew he wasn't good for me. I knew what I wanted and what he wanted, and it didn't match. Whenever I tried to end it *for good*, Nic would tell me exactly what I wanted to hear.

I would feel weak, always wanting and needing what he had to offer. Each time I said yes, I felt rewarded because we had so much fun together.

Just like any drug, I was on such a high when I was with him, and then I would crash and feel bad about myself when I wasn't with him. Nic held all the power, leaving me in constant anticipation, waiting for the next "hit" of connection.

I noticed a pattern: my client and money flow would dry up whenever I was entangled with him, even just wanting him. This created a cycle of dependence, where I would say yes to him to have a nice dinner and to help me with my business.

I became a victim, desperately seeking a savior. But when I mustered the strength to shut him out and reconnect with myself, I flourished.

The course leader's words, spoken during an intensive weekend workshop, echoed in my mind: "Your father is like cocaine to you. You're addicted to his love."

Driven by a deeply buried longing for my father's love, I consistently chose men who reflected him, and Nic was no exception. Their emotional abandonment only deepened my yearning and perpetuated the cycle.

Nic yelled at me, "Stop crying and stop being such a VICTIM." His emotional abuse hit me deep and hard. I immediately grabbed my things off the floor and ran down the stairs and out the door.

When I returned to my place, I swung open the door and slammed it behind me. I stumbled to the bathroom and collapsed on the cold tiles, my body shaking as I curled into a ball, heaving and crying. My stomach expanded, and yeast poured out of me.

That's when I knew my chronic symptoms were emotional.

For over two weeks before this night, I decided to eat close to the candida diet, again. I religiously woke up every morning and practiced Kundalini yoga. I finally knew it had nothing to do with my diet, parasites, or my perfect spiritual practice. *It had always been emotional.*

No diet, spiritual practice, or healer could fix what was hurting inside, the toxic patterns and the pain—it all stayed until I gave my inner child the emotional nurturance and support she was longing for all along.

Looking back, I can see how my relationship with my father shaped every romantic choice I made. The emotional wounds I carried from his unpredictable anger and emotional distance left me constantly seeking love and validation in men who mirrored those same patterns.

Nic wasn't the first, and he wouldn't be the last, but my entanglement with him became the turning point that forced me to confront the deeper roots of my pain.

This memoir isn't just about one relationship; it's about the lifelong cycle I was trapped in and how I finally found the courage to break free.

BAD BUNNY

After breaking off my engagement with Marc, I was heartbroken and lost. I left my loft for my usual comfort: wine and sushi. As I wandered through the doors of Whole Foods, the scent of sandalwood soap from a nearby kiosk overwhelmed the produce section. I stopped to compare apples, wondering if the organic green ones smelled any different from their glossy counterparts.

Abandoning my apple investigation, I glanced up, and there they were: *those eyes*. My ex-lover, Justin, stood on the other side of the grape display. A familiar intoxication swept over me. Butterflies erupted in my stomach; the world tilted on its axis.

At that moment, I wanted nothing more than to be with him. Blushing, I returned his greeting, "Hi."

He followed with "You look good, Elicia."

Swept away in the moment, I replied, "Thank you, you too, Justin."

I did look fantastic. Marc preferred me waif-thin with my hair down my back, so I became devoted to Pilates and my elliptical machine, walked my dog Hudson for miles a day, and ate an extremely strict diet. I achieved the "model shape" he desired, convincing myself it was what I wanted, too.

Gazing into Justin's mesmerizing blue eyes, I answered his question about my corporate sales job. "Great! I'm number three in the country for ADP TotalSource now."

When I inquired about his spa, he flashed that devilish grin and replied, "We were voted the number one spa in Atlanta."

I remember the first time I met Justin seven years ago in his spa. I walked in and introduced myself, "Hi, I'm Elicia, your new Paychex sales representative."

Justin gave me that same devilish smile and flirted with me, saying, "It's nice to meet you, Elicia. Come back later today, and I'll give you a massage." He scheduled me for the last appointment of the day, and what followed was an intensely passionate encounter on the massage table.

Afterward, still flushed and elated, we went to dinner, where Justin treated me to the seafood clay pot, one of the most delicious Thai dishes I'd ever tasted.

"Well, it's good to see you, Justin," I mumbled, dazed, as I drifted away from the produce section. I kept my recent breakup with Marc to myself. My friends and I referred to him as "Marc with a c." Both Justin and Marc changed their birth names to be more original. They were also well known in the Atlanta hip social scene.

I had to pause in front of the milk section and ask myself, "What am I even doing here?" My encounter with Justin had left me in a daze, shaken by a potent cocktail of emotions. Then I remembered: *sushi and wine, my go-to remedies for heartbreak.*

The last time I saw Justin was a few months before, outside a gourmet sushi restaurant. It was a brief but charged interaction after five years of silence. As I left the restaurant with my VP of Sales, Justin, surrounded by friends and smoke, glanced at my diamond ring.

"When's the big day?" he asked.

"Next summer," I replied.

"That's a long time," he questioned. "We should ..."

I quickly agreed, "Yeah, we should," and walked away, my heart pounding.

I returned to the present and navigated my way to the wine section. I grabbed my favorite cabernet and put it in my empty basket. At the sushi counter, I felt a presence behind me and turned. It was Justin.

"I'm addicted to you, Elicia," he said.

"I know," I replied. "I'm addicted to you, too."

He asked for my number and disappeared.

As I settled back at my loft, I sat at my desk to savor my sushi and wine. My gaze drifted out the window, where the iconic Bank of America building stood tall, its sparkly silhouette reminding me of a festive rocket.

At that moment, my phone pinged—a message from Justin. My heart skipped a beat. "I can't believe the timing of seeing you," I typed back. "I just broke off my engagement with Marc today."

He replied, "OMG, that's wild. I also just ended things with Nancy for good. I got my key back from her right before I saw you at Whole Foods."

We both realized it was fate. Justin asked, "The Four Seasons or The Ritz?"

I quickly replied, "The Ritz." We knew we couldn't be seen in public yet.

That night, our bodies were "Puttin' on the Ritz" with pure passion, lit with champagne, cocaine, and ecstasy. Justin's desire for me was palpable, a stark contrast to the performative nature of intimacy with Marc.

Where Marc required lace, garter belts, and practiced seduction, Justin wanted me wild and naked. His unfiltered passion ignited a hunger in me, filling a void that had long been empty. Sex and desire were my desperate attempts to feel loved and worthy of love.

After two weeks of being consumed by Justin's intoxicating passion, I returned Marc's ring. The following morning, nestled in the comfort of my loft, Justin turned to me and said, "I don't want to live without you, Elicia."

I said, "I don't want to live without you either, Justin."

His eyes lit up, and he said with a grin, "Let's go to Vegas today and get married. I'll take care of the hotel; you book the flights."

Everything magically fell into place. I cashed in my Delta SkyMiles for two first-class tickets, departing that evening. Justin, meanwhile, packed his stylish designer "wedding suit" and leather cowboy boots and confirmed our reservation at the luxurious Four Seasons in Vegas. We tossed a few essentials into a small bag, sealing our pact of secrecy. We didn't want anyone to tell us we were crazy.

We were both well-traveled, so during our flight, Justin suggested we marry somewhere neither of us had been. To our surprise, neither of us had been to the Grand Canyon.

"Let's take a helicopter over the canyon and get married!" Justin exclaimed with a sparkle in his eyes. As our plane descended into Vegas, the giant Neiman Marcus building caught my eye. "That's where I'll find my wedding dress," I said as a thrill ran through me.

We floated down to the pool the first morning, still buzzing from love and whatever substances we indulged in the night before. Sipping cocktails in our cozy poolside lounge, we gushed about our whirlwind romance to our waitress.

As Justin shared his helicopter wedding idea, she exclaimed, "Oh! I'm a wedding videographer, and my boyfriend owns HeliUSA. He flies people over the Grand Canyon for helicopter weddings."

At that moment, we hired them both on the spot for our wedding adventure the next day. It was so obvious that the Universe was supporting our fated destiny.

Neiman Marcus opened two hours before our limo picked us up. It was like a dream—I ran up the escalator and found the perfect dress, a sexy size four with a low v-neck, sparkling rhinestones, and a side slit for only $300.

While a Bobbi Brown makeup artist painted my face, Justin made a quick trip to Steve Madden and returned with a sly grin and a pair of white, five-inch heels. He loved that I was tall—all six feet of me—even though he was a few inches shorter.

We looked and acted like rock stars. It's a funny coincidence that Renée Zellweger and Kenny Chesney also eloped around the same time and annulled around the same time, too.

Arm in arm, we practically skipped with excitement toward the helicopter. Justin put his hands around my waist as he helped me up the metal steps in those five-inch heels.

As we put on our headsets, we laughed and kissed, the taste of Veuve Clicquot still sparkling on our tongues. I nestled my head on his shoulder, inhaling the familiar scent of hair gel and tobacco—a strangely intoxicating combination.

The helicopter lifted, and I let out a "WHOO" with exhilaration as we soared over the Grand Canyon. Gazing down at the majestic expanse, I understood the meaning of "Grand" in a visceral way. A rush of adrenaline surged through me.

As I took a deep breath, I felt an overwhelming sense of expansiveness within myself and the vastness surrounding us. At that moment, we were on top of the world, closer than ever.

Our private wedding ceremony took place on a remote, deserted ranch in Arizona. The officiant, sporting badass cowboy boots, lit a cigarette and said we could choose any location. With a mischievous glint in his eye, Justin declared he knew the perfect spot.

Later that night, as I drifted off to sleep with my head on Justin's chest, a chilling memory surfaced: saying "I do" below the noose on the ranch. Justin had chosen the platform where they used to hang people for our vows, laughing as he declared, "This is where we will tie the knot."

I dismissed it as a quirky joke, but a shiver of doubt ran through me. *Was it a morbid premonition?* I pushed the unsettling thought away, burying it deep beneath a layer of denial. I couldn't let my doubts get in the way of my happy facade for our grand return.

The following night, I was alone in the hotel hallway in total shock. Just moments before, Justin had erupted and hurled his phone against the wall, kicked me out of our room, and threatened to call his divorce attorney.

My heart sank as I glanced at the text message from Will flashing on my phone: "Say it ain't so ..." We had just returned to our room after poolside drinks, and the timing couldn't have been worse.

I shared the text from Will with Justin without considering our earlier conversation. At the pool, Justin had asked if I still spoke to Will, my former "friend with benefits." He and Will were rivals, and he wanted to be sure Will wasn't in my life. I told him I had stopped talking to Will when I started dating Marc.

When I saw Will's text, all that mattered was the realization that our elopement was out. Will's text confirmed that my best friend had drowned her disbelief in alcohol and told Will, even though I hadn't spoken to him in two years.

In Justin's mind, Will's text message was proof that I lied to him and was "still fu**ing Will." Nothing I said to explain it was heard over his screaming rage.

Outside our hotel room door, I took a deep, shaky breath, knowing I had made a horrific mistake. I needed to prove to myself I hadn't, so I completely forgot about the abuse.

Knock knock, can I come in? Rolling around in the sheets all night made it all better, as it always did.

I was born with an innately high emotional intelligence. To cope with my dad's anger and scary questions like, "Who did this?" I responded with, "Shame—me did it." I was essentially naming the emotion and putting it outside myself in a pretend friend, similar to the movie *Inside Out*.

Even at four years old, I possessed a fierce sense of justice, a primal urge to stand up to abuse. When my dad's rage erupted, directed at my mother, I would scream for him to stop.

But my mother, drawing from her childhood experiences, taught me a different lesson: to suppress my instincts, to "let it go," to bury the pain and pretend it never happened.

Since my mother was out of touch with her emotions, my very first sentence was, "Don't cry, baby." Throughout my childhood, my emotional hurt was met with, "Oh, Eli, you're too sensitive."

This ingrained pattern, a toxic cycle of recognition and denial, played on repeat for nearly two decades. *This is abuse*, a voice within me would cry. *This is wrong. Make it stop. Make him understand.*

But my mother's voice, the voice of self-preservation, would quickly drown it out. *Forget about it, disconnect from the pain and your knowing. Don't think about it. It's in the past.* I would unconsciously disconnect from my feelings, even when the abuse still hung heavy in the air.

Back in Atlanta, the town buzzed with gossip, and we were caught up in our intense passion. Within the first month, Justin gave me a two-carat diamond ring, which I laughed about with my coworkers. "This must be a first. I've had two different two-carat diamond rings on my finger in one month."

We decided to get artistically designed tattoos together, a permanent reminder of our bond. After only two months, we decided to buy a brand new house, with plans to move in the following month.

At the time, Justin was a paranoid, undiagnosed bipolar narcissist. I didn't see anyone else while we were together; it was just me and him at the house every night.

I was at the top of my company in corporate sales, and he didn't like it. He wanted me to stay home and not work. Our late-night partying definitely affected me at my job, and people noticed I wasn't the same.

I won President's Club again that year, but the prize—a trip to London—turned into a nightmare as I hid in the hotel bathroom, trying to protect myself from Justin's rage.

For a brief, terrifying moment, his abuse became physical. Justin busted down the bathroom door where I was hiding, grabbed me by my throat, threw me down on the bed, and left.

I was traumatized and devastated, but instead of even thinking for one moment of leaving him, I craved connecting with him. Instead of enjoying the trip I had won, I lay on the bed, heaving and crying in the dark all day because he wasn't answering my calls.

Justin called me later that night from another hotel room he got—I missed him so much. We never talked about what happened; we just resumed our addiction to each other with lots of sex. In our drunken bliss, we called the airline to change our tickets. *We are having the best time; let's stay a little longer.*

But later that night, Justin unleashed his rage on me again. At that moment, my self-preservation kicked in. I fled to our original hotel room and immediately changed my flight back to leave that day without telling Justin.

On the plane, my coworkers stared at me with concern and disapproval. They thought I was lying when I told them Justin was staying in London because he was sick. Well, I wasn't lying. He was mentally sick. *Very.*

Justin's biggest fear was abandonment, and I left him on another continent. When I got home, I was scared for my life. I called my mom to talk to her and reassure myself, "It's okay. He's just like Dad, so I know how to handle him."

She wasn't too concerned; she always knew I was stronger than her.

Did it get worse when he returned?

It was hard to say, but he didn't physically abuse me again. The next two weeks were a blend of our typical fleeting moments of fun and inevitable late-night rage.

One evening, after a long day at work, I opened the door to our house. As I entered the hallway, something cracked under my high heel. The air felt cold, and my breath caught in my throat. *Where is he? What's happening?*

Dread coiled in my stomach. I didn't know what awaited me, but terror pulsed through me. My hypervigilance kicked in, and I quickly scanned the room.

New locks were on the kitchen counter, waiting to be installed. Justin had started a list on a pad of my "failures" during his one-night absence.

1. Didn't pick me up from the airport.
2. Didn't pack up the house.

The list went on, but by #2, I was trembling. My eyes darted around the room, taking in the damage. Our framed wedding certificate lay shattered on the hallway floor.

Across the room, my painting titled "Bad Bunny"— a housewarming gift commissioned by Will and painted by my artist friend Bethany—had been violently keyed and discarded.

Total survival mode kicked in, and I scanned the entire house to see what I could quickly pack to get out as soon as possible. While frantically gathering my clothes from the dryer in the basement, I heard Justin come home.

As I carefully reached the top of the stairs, I peeked around the corner to see if I was safe and saw him waiting for me. He was holding my PF Chang's leftover box. As I entered the kitchen, Justin threw it against the wall, screaming, "WHO DID YOU FUCK?"

I calmly replied, "I had lunch by myself during work, and you are crazy." Justin raised his fist and said, "You wanna see crazy?!" As I stared at the shattered things on the floor, I replied, "I already did." He left abruptly.

I called my best friend, Liz, and begged her to help me pack as much as we could fit in our cars for a quick escape, including my sweet yellow lab, Hudson, who had to endure all of this daily verbal and emotional abuse as well.

Liz asked me a reasonable question: "What if he kills us both?" I matter-of-factly said, "That's the risk you are going to have to take, Liz." *I am eternally grateful for the risk she took for me.*

As we were backing our cars out of the driveway, Justin roared up on his motorcycle. He approached my window, clutching a wine bottle in each hand. His eyes held a pleading desperation as he begged, "Don't do this, Elicia."

My mind started to play tricks on me, so I turned to Liz and asked her if I was making the right decision. She firmly said, "YES, let's go."

Thankfully, my loft hadn't been sold. I had my happy place back with Huddles, the dog who cuddles. Hudson gave me the nurturance I so desperately needed.

That same week, Justin and I had to close on the house we had bought together. Our realtor felt so bad for us that he offered to sell it without a commission. Justin, wallowing in self-pity, refused. "Where else will I live?"

I retorted, "In any of the thousands of places for rent."

Out of spite, he moved into our house, and I was forced to pay a divorce attorney $10,000 to annul our three-month marriage and ensure he refinanced the mortgage into his name within six months.

One night, shortly after I left, he bombarded me with harassing and threatening messages, desperate for me to call back. He threatened to burn all my clothes in his front yard, but I ignored him because his neighbor confirmed that he was bluffing.

A jolt of fear woke me at three in the morning, and I looked at my phone. A stream of deranged text messages from Justin was pouring in:

I found your whore photos. Call me, or I will send them to everyone we know. I'm with Mike, and I am showing them to him.

I called his friend Mike immediately. "Mike, what in the hell is he talking about? I don't have any printed photos of me naked or with anyone else, and we deleted all our photos from our devices when we got married."

Mike sounded genuinely worried. "Justin's losing it," he said, his voice strained. "He's shaking and crying. He found a couple of photos of you and Will having sex on your old Maxtor hard drive."

Holy shit, Will! Justin was so convinced I was having an affair that he actually found a hidden photo I wasn't even aware of, from five years prior, of me with his nemesis!

Nausea twisted my stomach as I checked my email. *Oh my God, he actually did it.* In my inbox were copies of every email he'd sent. He simply hit "reply all" on our wedding party invitation list, exposing the photo to all our friends and family with the subject line: "My wife with another man." He even sent it to my ex-fiancé, Marc, with the subject line: "Thought you should know."

Somewhat relieved, I texted Justin, "Well, at least now I don't need to explain to everyone why I left you."

Fearful for my safety and unsure of what he might do next, I called the police the next day to file a report. I explained how long we had known each other, that we had been married for three months, and detailed the events surrounding my departure and the email he'd sent to practically everyone we knew. The photo had spread across Atlanta.

A month later, Liz's frantic call sent a chill down my spine. "Oh, Woodford." I've heard that alarming tone before in her voice and knew something was very wrong. She sighed, "Your police report is in the Blotter."

My heart sank. "Oh no," I breathed, dread washing over me. *Creative Loafing* was a popular Atlanta publication, and its "Blotter" section, a collection of humorous police reports, was widely read.

Both Liz and I knew how Justin would react. As predicted, he left me a furious message, accusing me of intentionally using the Blotter to destroy his reputation. He raged that all his clients read it and knew it was about him. Of course, he could only blame me rather than face the reasons why I had to file that report *after* I left him.

Shortly after his message, I spiraled into my first depression. My emotions, once suppressed, overwhelmed me. I collapsed on the couch in the middle of the day, unable to cope.

For the first time in my life, I turned inward and asked myself, *What made me do that? What made me choose him and all of them?* I knew I needed help. This was the beginning of my awakening to self-awareness.

While married to Justin, I remembered a friend of his who told me about a transformative weekend workshop she attended. She seemed completely changed afterward. I contacted her for information about the course. They offered weekend and year-long workshops with experiential processes to heal subconscious patterns from childhood.

I enrolled in the first available course, which took place the month after my divorce Freedom Party.

MILLION-DOLLAR DIAMOND

On a crisp fall Friday evening, I parked my fast silver Saab and took in the colorful foliage that carpeted the ground. Stepping toward the door, I took a deep breath of the crisp air. I felt nervous excitement for what lay ahead.

I strode confidently into the center, my designer white corduroy pants and black leather cowboy boots adding a certain swagger. A soft-spoken woman guided nine other students and me into a single file as we entered the classroom.

I scanned the room, noting the warm smiles of those who had already completed the course and were now present to assist us as "angels"—two assigned to each student. My angels were two men who, at first glance, seemed a little less lost than me.

Leaders in front of us, angels to the back, stuck in the middle of the room. Song lyrics are constantly spinning and morphing into new, Weird Al-esque versions in my head. It's one of my favorite ways to play—my silly, creative little girl always finding a way to express herself.

My playful little girl wasn't out yet, though. She was hiding under a picture-perfect shell of Bobbie Brown makeup, $400 highlights, freshly waxed eyebrows, and my first boob job.

The leader possessed an almost uncanny ability to write personalized intentions for each of us before meeting us. Given that I'd provided minimal information on the course form—omitting any mention of Justin—I was surprised and confused when I heard mine.

Form a new identity
Be your own authority
You are the leader.

When she asked me, "If you had a million-dollar diamond, would you lose it?"

I simply replied, "I don't like diamonds."

Later, finding myself in the "hot seat" for analysis, I began by expressing that I felt sorry for those who had endured horrific childhoods, as mine had been happy.

With seasoned wisdom, the leader recognized the futility of challenging my heavily armored defenses at that point. Instead, she observed as I sat off to the side, restlessly kicking one foot over the other, chewing gum, and flipping my perfectly styled hair like a petulant teenager.

She inquired, "Do you know what an empowered woman is?"

"Of course!" I retorted. "I come from a long line of empowered women. My mom has five sisters who are very successful doctors and business owners, and my grandmother was a trailblazer in her field."

With a loving smile, she told me I had no idea what empowered meant. Those examples are all about proving and pining for approval.

As she said that, I glanced around the room and my eyes landed on a gorgeous angel assistant with long brown hair and big, deep brown eyes. This woman was sitting straight in her chair, penetrating me with a certain confidence and inner power that was unfamiliar to me. *Was this what empowerment looked like?*

The weekend was filled with experiential therapy, designed to open us up to heal the source of our problematic patterns, awaken our true self, and move toward our heart's desires.

During my individual process, the leader instructed me to close my eyes and find my little girl. In the darkness behind my eyelids, I saw a photo of me when I was five years old, a very sweet and painfully shy flower girl at my godmother's wedding. My pink dress was too small, but I insisted on wearing it.

The leader deeply encouraged me to be the parent my inner child needs, to make good decisions for her, and to love and accept her.

"Open your eyes, Elicia." When I opened my eyes, I looked at myself in the mirror and stared at Eli (pronounced Ellie), my inner child, feeling and loving her.

After the course, I knew exactly what to do with the large tattoo outline on my back—the one I'd gotten with

Justin. I had it shaded in to look like a mirror because I found myself through him.

This deeply altering weekend changed my entire life. I wondered, *What else don't I know?*

Determined to heal my subconscious childhood patterns and release anything false, I committed to taking all the courses offered and dedicating myself to assisting as an angel every month for four years.

After that first weekend, I felt my inner child next to me. Holding her hand, I started to question my choices and habits. For the first time, I decided not to go out to get drunk to bring some random guy home.

Instead, I stayed in and drank a bottle of wine alone. Learning to be alone was challenging, surrounded by temptation and friends who invited me out to bars and restaurants every night. *I'm lonely* would creep into my thoughts.

Rather than believing these thoughts, I countered them. *No, Elicia, you aren't lonely. Only five minutes ago, you told your friends you wanted to stay in tonight.*

I recognized the two paths before me: believing everything my mind told me would lead to the bar and away from my inner child, the other toward self-connection and healing.

I was embarking on the long, winding, foggy road to becoming my own authority.

A month after my first course, I spent Christmas with my family in San Francisco. The distance from my Atlanta drama felt so liberating that I decided to relocate. My brother already lived there, and a friend of a friend from Atlanta was also moving to my desired neighborhood.

Every man I encountered before moving had significant mommy issues that they projected onto me. My response was to refer them to the course. For years, I jokingly believed my sole purpose with men was to send them there, earning me the nickname "the course whisperer."

With my annulment from Justin finalized, I searched for a tenant for my loft as I prepared to move to San Francisco. A couple who lived next door, whom I'd also referred to the course, invited me to a black-tie event.

As it turned out, they secretly fixed me up with their tall, handsome friend. "Hi, I'm Elicia."

His eyes smiled back, "Hi, I am Chris."

We hit it off right away. I made it clear, though, that I did not want a relationship and would be moving to San Francisco soon.

Two weeks later, we were enjoying Thai food and wine in my loft, casually discussing our careers. When I mentioned Paychex, he responded with his company's name. I totally freaked out. Dropping my fork, I bolted across the room in shock.

It turned out that Chris and I had had a one-night stand seven years earlier when I was moving to NYC—a fact neither of us remembered until two weeks into our current relationship.

The only two clients I'd ever been involved with were Justin and Chris, and fate had reconnected me with both of them seven years later. *I had to get out of here.*

Wherever you go, there you are.

Broken and exhausted after a year of struggle in San Francisco, I found myself counting down the days until my lease ended, eager to move back to Atlanta.

As the wind whipped through my hair, I felt a sense of liberation as I drove Hudson and my essentials over the Bay Bridge, heading back to my Atlanta loft—my sanctuary.

The entire year in San Francisco was incredibly challenging. While I planned my move with the understanding that "seven years prior" Chris would rent my loft, his commitment was merely a manipulation tactic to keep me in a relationship.

When he visited me in San Francisco, I sent him back to Atlanta and straight to the course, where he ultimately met his future wife.

Shortly after moving to San Francisco, I was burdened with both my Atlanta loft mortgage and rent in one of the most expensive cities. The financial strain worsened when I discovered a delinquency on my credit report a few months later.

Justin had stopped making payments on the house we'd bought together—the one I never moved into. To avoid foreclosure, I had to cover three months of back payments on the expensive property, all while Justin remained indifferent to the consequences of bankruptcy. Ultimately, I had to force the sale of the house.

Despite a promotion and bonus for opening four new Bay Area offices for ADP TotalSource, I remained overwhelmed by debt and living beyond my means. Though drowning in bills, I clung to hope.

A miraculous business opportunity landed in my lap, promising a commission far beyond my wildest dreams. I poured every ounce of energy into it, using the work to escape the emotional pain I'd begun to uncover through the course.

Adderall was my savior, keeping me awake and somewhat focused as I fueled my late nights with two bottles of wine, working until three in the morning.

One rainy morning, while walking Hudson in Mission Dolores Park, I received devastating news from my boss. After three months of nonstop work on this deal, just as it was about to close, my neglectful manager informed me that we couldn't proceed due to high-risk health insurance cases.

Like Hudson's playful rolls, I collapsed onto the muddy grass, but mine was with dread. *NO WAY! This was going to solve all my problems. I HAD to make it happen.*

Trudging back to my apartment, covered in mud and despair, I said to myself in jest, *If I don't get this deal, I'm going to file for bankruptcy, sell everything I own, and move to Thailand.*

Another cross-country drive provided the clarity I needed. I realized that a business deal wouldn't solve my problems—I had to take responsibility. *Clean up the mess you created, Elicia.*

The path forward was clear: move back to my loft until it sold, find another job, and enroll in the 18-month course at the center.

At the end of the course, I was given this intention:

> *Take it one step at a time on the long journey of the path of Spirit. Get focused with a beginner's mind, past the identities that have their "way of rightness." Grow into maturity with a true mastery, based on being deeply grounded and devoted to listening, to the embracing of truth within. Then, in the empty mystery, you will birth the heart mother that nurtures the spirit of all.*
>
> *To encourage others to live the beauty of their Spirits FULLY! To help them break through restrictions to FULL ALIVENESS.*

Each experiential weekend was subtle yet intense, altering my reality. One particularly memorable weekend focused on singing. We each chose a meaningful song lyric and sang it for hours, allowing its truth to resonate within us. As George Michael's "Freedom" played, the lyrics struck a new chord, contrasting the perfection I strived for and the genuine self I longed to embrace.

I struggled with the song, becoming increasingly frustrated with each mistake. The theme of "disappointment" emerged during the first weekend, revealing my subconscious pattern of operating from a fear of disappointing others.

As I grappled with my chosen song, the group leaders highlighted my underlying need for perfection. This newfound awareness and a burning desire for change inspired me to create my own song.

I can't be perfect because I am me
I can't be perfect because I'm free
I am free
I am free
I am free
To be me.

Each of us had to sing our song, standing in the middle of the circle of students sitting while they clapped. I was wearing all black that day. The leader told me to go last.

As I stood in the middle, the leader silenced the clapping. She recognized my inner strength and knew I needed to be truly heard. My song expanded, growing in power and connection as I circled the group, singing directly to each person, eye to eye.

I can't be perfect because I am me
I can't be perfect because I'm free
I am free
I am free
I am free
To be me.

And you are free
And you are free
And you are free
To be you.

And I love you
And I love you
And I love you
And you too.

After the singing weekend, I contracted a severe case of the flu. It felt like the need to be perfect was being purged from my cells, expelled through sweat and fever.

The new wave music that usually brought me joy was unbearable; its energy was too jarring for my sensitive nervous system. Only the soothing sounds of chanting and a custom sound frequency provided relief and helped me realign my awareness.

The course leaders warned us that anything false would start to blow up, and they were right. As I began asserting my needs, a friend I consistently overgave to lashed out and accused *me* of selfishness. She abandoned me at our friend's wedding, leaving me to drive home alone for two hours, uncontrollably crying.

The day before my 33rd birthday, I sat at my desk, struggling to work on a proposal. Crafting proposals—once my favorite task, the gateway to sales, money, and achievement—now felt strange and unfulfilling. My soul ached, a feeling of profound misalignment.

In tears, I walked out of the office, driven solely by my emotions. While driving home, I instinctively called my boss: "I quit."

Despite having no savings, I felt no urgency to plan my next move. Since my birthday is on the first of December, I gave myself a gift: I would take the entire month to detox my corporate life and identity. I purged all traces of that life, including binders and books, and permanently deleted files.

Near the end of December, an email newsletter caught my attention. A small note at the bottom seemed to speak directly to my soul: "Do you want to empower others to know themselves, to deeply connect with and take care of themselves?"

A few months before leaving my corporate job, the name "ePowerMe" popped into my head while driving. I pulled over and jotted it down, sensing its potential as a business name. I brainstormed a few taglines:

ePowerMe

Elicia will empower you.

Become empowered with Elicia.

Elicia will help you find the power within you.

YES, I want to empower others to know themselves. Tell me more! I clicked the link from Higher Awareness and found the offering "Become a Journaling Facilitator." It resonated with me deeply.

Ironically, we were encouraged to journal about our feelings during the 18-month course at the center. Staring at the blank page, I could only think about how much I disliked journaling.

Because I had an aversion to it, I decided to enroll and become a journaling facilitator. After signing up, I received a hefty set of binders filled with journaling techniques. The intensive training required daily journaling, utilizing 100 different techniques over three months.

As I developed my own "Journaling for Self-Awareness" workshops, I experienced a profound sense of joy and fulfillment—a natural high that surpassed any other. I even stopped drinking, unwilling to disrupt this newfound sense of well-being.

My family, however, was not supportive. Every phone call with my mom, dad, or brother included the same worried question: "When are you going to get a job?"

They treated me like I was a homeless addict, completely disregarding my happiness. It dawned on me that my father's past assurances of unconditional support, "You can do anything you want," actually meant, "You can do anything I approve of, as long as it comes with a large paycheck."

What was I supposed to do?

TWO WORLDS

It was incredibly fulfilling to lead journaling exercises in my living room that connected people to their hearts. To further support the journey of self-discovery, I created workbooks for self-awareness designed to guide others toward inner clarity and well-being.

With my intuitive sense for marketing, I quickly recognized that Facebook, a new social media platform, had the potential to revolutionize event promotion.

I leveraged the platform exclusively to market my workshops and created a local holistic community, connecting people with valuable wellness resources.

As a result, Atlanta-based holistic businesses and practitioners sought my expertise in social media marketing. While my income from journaling workshops and online marketing consulting was steady, it wasn't enough to maintain my previous lifestyle or cover my bills.

Each ring of the phone sent a wave of dread through me. Credit card companies hounded my landline, their endless voicemails a constant reminder of my financial failures. The reality of my situation was inescapable: I couldn't pay my mortgage, and I was sinking into a deep, dark depression.

Upon opening my eyes each morning, I was unable to stand. I found myself on the floor, curled up in a ball, sobbing and trembling. I couldn't straddle the crack of my two worlds anymore. My high crashed, and reality set in. I wanted to die.

In a state of despair, I shared my struggles on Facebook. An angel appeared: Julia from my holistic community. She offered me her visualization program.

For ten minutes each day, I would close my eyes and immerse myself in a vision of my ideal life: working with health retreats on a serene island in Thailand. It was pure bliss. The phone would ring, another collector, and I doubted how I could get out of the mess I had made.

My family kept asking, "When are you going to get a job?" Clinging desperately to my loft, Saab, and material possessions, I applied for sales jobs, waited tables, and borrowed money to pay my mortgage.

The weight of insurmountable credit card debt, coupled with the housing market crash that left me underwater on my mortgage and car loan, finally forced me to surrender. I decided to file for bankruptcy.

Letting it all go gave me a new sense of freedom. It was a light bulb moment of exhilarating relief. *If I don't have any bills, I don't need a job here ... I can actually move to Thailand!*

A smile crossed my face as I remembered making that same declaration three years earlier in a San Francisco park: *If I don't get this deal, I will file bankruptcy, sell everything I own, and move to Thailand.* Now, it seemed, that jest had become my reality.

My mom came to visit and join me in another course. After a deeply revealing weekend, we walked through the sliding doors of Whole Foods. The familiar scent of overpriced produce and woodsy soaps enveloped me. Suddenly, a parody song by DJ Dave, "Whole Foods Parking Lot," one of my new favorites, played in my head. *It sure was getting real.*

I shared the good news with my mom, "I've decided to move to Thailand."

Totally shocked, she responded, "WHAT?! How will you pay back the money you borrowed from your aunt?"

I yelled, "You don't support my happiness or my ability to make money; you're just living in fear."

Despite the initial conflict, I have to give Mom credit; she reflected on it and has supported my choices ever since.

She did have a point, though. How *was* I going to repay the borrowed money and bankruptcy attorney fees?

My neighbor mentioned a new club opening nearby that was hiring cocktail servers. I had to tap back into the old, fading version of myself to finally shed that identity. I hustled, not for material gain, but for my freedom and true calling.

FASTING AND EXCRETION

My "Thai One On" going-away party with friends was a joyous send-off. The next day, I packed two enormous pink suitcases with my life that I was bringing with me to Thailand. I'd spent the past month simplifying, selling, and giving away everything I owned.

As I prepared for Thailand, I was filled with an exhilarating sense of freedom. "How long are you going for?" was on repeat, but I had no answer. I was stepping into the unknown, guided only by Spirit.

Upon arrival, I soon realized that most businesses in Thailand desperately needed internet marketing assistance. I decided to offer trades with health resorts to immerse myself in the retreat lifestyle and experience the benefits of cleansing programs.

My initial trade involved setting up a Facebook account, blog, and newsletter for a Chiang Mai resort. The owner, a pioneer of detox retreats in Thailand, shared that he had opened the first detox health retreat on Koh Samui two decades prior.

I was floored when he said, "I created our seven-day juice fasting program based on my favorite book, *The Tao of Health, Sex, and Longevity.*"

Am I dreaming? Just a year ago, I woke up depressed and collapsed on the floor in tears, which led me to create a "mind movie" visualization of myself living on a Thai island and working with health retreats.

Now, here was the pioneer telling me that all the detox health retreats on Koh Samui, which also happened to be the name of my favorite Thai restaurant during my year in San Francisco, were based on *this* very book.

My obsession with detoxing and cleansing began at Marist College in Poughkeepsie, New York. My brother had given me the book *The Tao of Health, Sex, and Longevity,* which included a seven-day cleanse program. Now, the mere thought of that book and the absurd rules Daniel Reid outlined makes me cringe.

- Rule: Meat and milk must never be consumed at the same meal.
- Rule: Protein and starch are the worst possible combination of foods to mix in a single meal.
- Rule: Eat concentrated proteins such as meat, fish, eggs, and cheese separately from concentrated starches such as bread, potatoes, and rice.
- Rule: Eat only one major type of protein in a single meal. Avoid combinations such as meat and eggs, meat and milk, or fish and cheese.

- Rule: Eat starches and acids at separate meals. For example, if you eat toast or cereal for breakfast, skip the orange juice as well as eggs. If you're eating a starch-based meal of noodles or rice, avoid vinegar as well as concentrated protein.
- Rule: Avoid combining concentrated proteins and acids in the same meal.
- Rule: Eat concentrated proteins and fats at separate meals. When you cannot avoid mixing them, eat plenty of raw vegetables to assist their digestion and passage.
- Rule: Avoid consuming sugars and proteins at the same meal.
- Rule: Eat starches and sugars separately.
- Rule: Eat melons alone or leave them alone.
- Rule: Drink milk alone or leave it alone.

And much, much more!

When I first read it, I ate it up. I was already bulimic, and this fit so nicely into my need to control my food, striving to be perfect and as skinny as possible.

It went on to say, "Avoid extreme emotions of all kinds, especially as you grow older. Nothing drains energy from the body as rapidly nor disrupts the functional harmony of vital organs as completely as strong outbursts of emotion."

Emotions? What emotions? I was happy all the time. Some mornings, when I would wake up next to a strange man, I would just binge eat and throw up afterward to feel better. No strong emotions, check mark.

When I got to the chapter titled "Fasting and Excretion," I was hooked. He instructs everyone to do a seven-day juice fast while participating in a colon cleansing program.

During the fast, you drink powdered psyllium seed, bentonite clay, and a vitamin mix powder multiple times a day. You also administer two five-gallon colonics daily on a colema board, which is gravity-fed and not pumped.

The results will amaze you! I couldn't wait to clean out my body, get all those toxins out, and see that thick black rubbery stuff in the toilet. Back then, I wasn't ready to give up beer yet for a day, but the seed was planted.

I spent my twenties in Atlanta drinking, drugging, and detoxing. I was on a perfect schedule of Detox-Retox. Outside of my corporate sales job, I had two hobbies: partying at night and researching wellness during the day.

What cleansing supplement can I try now?

How many colonics should I do this month?

Will weekly chiropractic really fix my neck?

Acupuncture for my liver, yes!

Seven-Day Panchakarma Detox Retreat for $5,000 to eat rice and lentils that made my bloating worse, why not?

Raw food diet, yes!

Industrial wheatgrass juicer on my kitchen counter, yes!

My favorite fasting program was the Master Cleanser, but the maple syrup caused my yeast infections to get out of control. I asked my gynecologist what was causing my monthly yeast infections and UTIs. She replied, "Nothing. Some women are more susceptible, so you just need to take Diflucan for the rest of your life."

I left her office in tears, dumbfounded. *What did she just say? That is insane*, I thought. As I wiped the tears from my face, I swore to myself: *There must be something causing this, and I will find out.*

The candida diet books scientifically explain how antibiotics cause systemic candida. Okay, that made sense to me. As a child, I would get strep throat every year on my birthday and was put on antibiotics.

The books detail how antibiotics wipe out the good bacteria. By eating all forms of sugar, starch, and dairy, the "bad bacteria"/yeast fungus overgrow and produce many symptoms. *Ding, ding, ding!*

The candida diet became my new religion. Eliminate all sugars, starches, vinegar, fermented things, beer, wine, alcohol, antibiotics, acne medication, birth control pills ...

I continued taking the pill and drinking alcohol, but eliminated pizza, bread, and beer from my diet. These were significant changes, and they made a noticeable difference. My monthly yeast infections and UTIs disappeared, and I lost weight.

During my annual gynecologist appointment, the doctor expressed surprise that she hadn't seen me in a while. I shared the details of my diet and suggested she recommend it to other patients.

A blood analysis table was set up at my favorite health food store, so, of course, I wanted to try it out. Researching wellness excited me so much.

After pricking my finger, the practitioner revealed that I had systemic candida. Seeing the defeated look on my face, she comforted me with a solution: "Take this candida cleanser supplement, and it will go away."

———

When I arrived at the Chiang Mai retreat, I was extremely bloated. I was eager to see the results of the seven-day fasting program and raw food diet. Not eating, cleansing my colon, losing weight, and pursuing perfection made me feel incredible.

As my program was ending, the owner suggested Koh Samui as my next destination, assuring me that it aligned perfectly with my passions.

As fate would have it, a conference was scheduled at Kamalaya on Koh Samui right after my program ended, uniting all the key resources in one location. It was a sign, and I kept following them.

Despite the darkness outside as my plane landed, I felt my entire being light up. I just knew this was where I would live. I arranged to stay one night at Kamalaya Wellness Sanctuary and Holistic Spa, renowned as the best in Asia, the night before the conference. They offered me a room in exchange for an online write-up in my upcoming Samui Healing Retreat Directory.

Living on a Thai island, researching detox retreats and healing resources—this was my paradise. However, after a couple more seven-day fasts, I indulged in a glass of wine, and my candida flared up, leaving me bedridden with the flu and a yeast infection.

One of the practitioners I consulted for my research looked into my eyes and informed me that I had systemic candida. *Of course I did. I've been treating candida symptoms for years.* She advised me to stop drinking alcohol for an extended period, something I hadn't yet attempted, although I had gone off birth control pills a couple of years prior.

I finally acknowledged my problem and committed to doing whatever it took to fully heal my candida. The next day, someone gave me Donna Gates' book, *The Body Ecology Diet*, which introduced me to new concepts that I believed held the answers I'd been missing. With its even stricter rules, I adopted what I dubbed "The Anti-Pleasure Diet."

Two years on that tropical Thai island were devoid of booze, fruit, rice, and pleasure—I was even detoxing my desire for sex. My nights were solitary, spent obsessively devouring books on health, healing, and spirituality.

When another holistic practitioner identified my mind as my primary stressor, I embarked on a ten-day silent meditation retreat. On day seven, I observed my mind spiraling into anxiety over the thought of losing my hair, and I recognized my attachment to it. At that moment, I knew I had to shave my head. I did so on New

Year's Eve and felt a connection to my true self for the first time.

During those awkward years between twelve and fourteen, I convinced myself that being skinny, tan, and having big boobs and long hair was the key to feeling good about myself.

So, I began growing my hair out and frequenting tanning beds. I even asked my mom if I could go on the pill—not for birth control, but because I'd heard it could increase breast size.

At that point, I only had slightly raised nipples. In junior high, when a teacher asked about flat lands, a boy in my class shouted, "Woodford." That shaming experience, buried deep within my subconscious, would later trigger my desire for breast implants when I was twenty-one.

A couple of years after that flatlands imprint, I experienced another defining moment that triggered my eating disorder. During high school basketball practice, my coach overheard us talking about another player's body, and in passing, he casually remarked, "Woodford, you are not skinny."

Although I wasn't overweight, I was devastated. That's when I became a "health nut" as a way to mask my disordered eating and body image issues.

This obsession eventually led me to pursue modeling, but even after becoming alarmingly thin, the agency still pushed me to lose more weight. During a college Christmas break, I visited my high school, and my coach told me I was too skinny. Go figure.

On this tropical island paradise, my mornings began with a scooter ride to a health resort for a green juice, followed by a sunrise beach walk and a swim.

During those walks, I often thought, *This is my ideal life.* As I zipped around the island on my Honda Scoopy, I'd laugh at the sight of monkeys tossing coconuts into workers' trucks in exchange for bananas.

"Sawadee kaaaaa," I'd greet everyone with a smile and a prayer bow, embracing the warmth of Thailand, the land of a thousand smiles. The low cost of living allowed me to enjoy all my meals at the resort's restaurant and indulge in a two-hour Thai massage a few times a week. Even though the smell is repugnant to most people, I would sometimes binge on the luscious durian fruit.

The Anti-Pleasure Diet seemed to make my bulimia worse, and I felt so ashamed. I thought, *I am a bulimic health retreat consultant with candida expertise, teaching people self-awareness while cleansing and being a hypocrite.* I kept researching.

As I was waking up one morning, I actually heard a voice in my head that said *Medical Intuitive*. Not thinking too much about it, I picked up my journal and wrote it down.

Later that day, my energy healer friend invited me to dinner with a client of hers who was leaving the next day. During dinner, her friend said, "I have another take on candida from Laura, my Medical Intuitive." *Whoa, okay, that's it.*

I booked a reading immediately. Laura opened my eyes to see the emotional and spiritual causes of candida.

The emotional aspect was about me needing to cleanse my guilt and shame. "You also need to learn to become an untamed wildfire," she said. "Holding back your purpose and passion is dampening your fire." I had no idea what she meant or what to do, but it kept me open to other possibilities.

Word of my candida crusade had spread among the island's practitioners. One day, a chiropractor with channeling abilities aggressively confronted me in a coffee shop, screaming, "WHAT IS CAUSING IT?!"

The encounter shook me deeply, and I felt compelled to take my only vacation off the island, seeking refuge on the smaller island of Koh Tao. The message, however jarringly delivered, resonated within me and lingered in my thoughts.

One day at a health resort, I met a woman who specialized in emotional healing. Over green juice, we connected, and I intuitively knew I needed to work with her, especially since our paths kept crossing.

When I finally earned enough money for a session, I confided in her about my binging and purging, a shameful secret I had kept hidden for thirty-six years.

After a week of releasing my repressed anger—screaming into pillows on the couch, in the ocean, and even while riding my scooter—I felt transformed. My perspective shifted, and a part of my ego identity dissolved.

The compulsion to preach detoxification to everyone vanished; in fact, I wanted to banish the word "detox" from my vocabulary entirely, despite having created a

Detox Retreat Directory on my new website, *Retreat Yourself to Be Yourself*.

I participated in a couple of Family Constellation sessions to reopen my heart to love. While I had believed I was happier alone, I realized I had closed myself off to protect myself from past pain.

After a period of intense grieving, I found myself floating in the ocean one night, gazing at the stars. In that moment, I felt a longing for my soulmate and a readiness for love.

During my second constellation, the facilitator revealed that the love I would find would be nothing like my parents had been. It became clear that I needed to leave the island; I was ready for a new chapter. Again, I trusted my intuition and followed the signs.

I confided in Ange, a soul sister and one of my dearest friends from San Francisco, about my desire to leave. We even got matching "Creative Goddess" tattoos in Haight-Ashbury just before I moved to Thailand—a design I found on a candle box that has since gained profound meaning.

Missing each other deeply, she immediately offered her couch as a place to crash. The timing perfectly aligned with my brother's fortieth birthday party, a clear sign pointing me forward.

I moved back to San Francisco. *My soul must really like to suffer*, I thought, leaving my island paradise to land amidst the chaos of Occupy Oakland protests.

The transition was jarring: from affordable to exorbitant, tropical heat to bone-chilling cold, serene health retreats to the harsh reality of homelessness. And to top it off, I was now back within reach of my family and all of my destabilizing emotional triggers.

I resorted to what I knew best to make money, securing a job as a server in a high-end restaurant. But darkness came over me once more, leading to heavy drinking and a longing for death.

Lost in this despair, I had lunch with a kindred spirit who was passing through—a man who had followed a similar path as mine in Thailand around the same time on the neighboring island of Koh Phangan. We had both developed journaling exercises to support people undergoing cleansing programs.

As soon as I sat down and looked into his big, brown, loving eyes, I broke down crying and confessed that it was all too hard. I would never kill myself, but I was praying not to live anymore because I didn't see the point. The suffering was too much.

He said, "Elicia, you are one of the most inspiring people I know. I love your Detox World Tour videos. You need to do those again; don't stop."

I partnered with an online holistic directory to foster community connection. This provided me with enough money for food, and I was pet sitting to keep a roof over my head.

Working with incredible healers, I exchanged marketing consulting for their services, which was crucial during this challenging time. Not only did this support my healing, but creating YouTube videos to share these healers' offerings kept me connected to my heart and purpose. I remain deeply grateful for this experience and his encouragement.

One night, while reading a book by one of the practitioners, the author's account of repressed sexual abuse triggered my own buried trauma.

Suddenly, I craved a cigarette, even though I didn't smoke. Instead, I turned to my familiar coping mechanism: binging and purging.

Afterward, I found myself on the floor, sobbing and begging for God to take me. "What is the meaning of my life?" I cried out in despair.

Emotions—I still didn't know anything about my intense emotions. The woman I worked with in Thailand came to mind, but I couldn't afford a session.

The next day, another practitioner from the community reached out. Tanya offered a Healing Activation Session in exchange for potential marketing help. I agreed, but went in with no expectations for the session itself.

After an hour of energy healing, she gently asked if I had ever experienced childhood sexual abuse. A visceral knowing resonated within me—it was true.

When I returned to the house where I was dog sitting, I began trembling uncontrollably and collapsed on the bed, my body convulsing as it released years of suppressed trauma. *How many times have I been violated in different ways?*

Shortly after, I saw a post from Veenaa, a shamanic healer, offering her Dances of Shakti, a deep trance journeywork with drumming followed by counseling. We arranged a three-hour in-person shamanic journey.

Veenaa created a personalized playlist for me, and during the session, I danced, expressed myself, and engaged in a mirror work process. We completed the journey with a meditation as she anointed me as a priestess.

Veenaa also shared her intuitive insight that, on a soul level, the sexual abuse helped me to not be involved with men for a significant period to fully embark on my journey of self-discovery and my purpose without distractions.

The next day, another practitioner in the community told me about a free talk on water fasting. The speaker was very convincing about how his 30-day water fast was the key to healing. *Okay, yeah, I haven't tried a pure water fast yet; maybe that is the missing ingredient—to not take any nutrients in for self-healing.*

He needed a YouTube channel, so I traded with him as my last experiment on my Detox World Tour. This was also my way out of my hell in San Francisco to retreat to the Costa Rican jungle. I felt a strong craving to connect more deeply with myself, in order to fully understand and heal from the newly discovered abuse.

PORTAL HORSE

Six weeks of self-imposed starvation in a Costa Rican jungle hammock ended with a flight back to Atlanta. It was exactly three years to the day since I had embarked on my "Detox World Tour."

As the city lights came into view, I realized this was my fifth time returning. *Surely*, I thought, *there must be a reason I keep coming back here.*

Nic saw my videos on YouTube while I was in Costa Rica and hired me to work on a wellness project in Atlanta. Even though I didn't want to return to the US, I was out of money and options, so I said yes.

When I saw Nic's picture on Facebook, something about his energy grabbed me and pulled me in. When we spoke, I felt a strong, familiar connection. There were many synchronicities, and I shared with him that it seemed we had a soul contract. Our connection was undeniable.

Right after I left Costa Rica, I spent a month at my aunt and uncle's house in New Jersey, visiting my dog, Hudson, whom I had given to them when I moved to Thailand. It was just me and Hudson for an entire month while they vacationed in Europe. My heart had broken when I left him; it was an important time for us to reconnect.

Hudson and I did all our favorite things together again. We took long walks through the beautiful Jersey suburban development. I threw his ball with the Chuckit! stick repeatedly until his big yellow Labrador body flopped down on the grass in exhaustion. We spent a lot of time loving each other on the living room carpet. Huddles, the dog who cuddles.

One evening, while sitting on the front step watching the sunset in the distance with Hudson by my side, I reflected on my 30-day water fast in Costa Rica. I found myself in a conflicting situation during the water fast with our leader.

Things were not as they seemed, and the three other women and I were vulnerable and depleted. On the one hand, I loved my spiritual connection during the fast and my slim body from losing thirty pounds.

On the other hand, we were all subjected to the leader's daily aggressive brainwashing lectures about how all foods and herbs are toxic except fruit.

During his lectures, I would point my finger toward the sky for the others to remember to rise above the energy coming at us. *It really is a jungle out there in the healing world.*

During my alone time with Hudson, I was detoxing the leader's energy, and my bulimia flared up. I spoke with Nic about his wellness project. Through our text messages, we had a very strong psychic connection. I was intrigued. Our messages were mentally stimulating and deep. We both felt we already knew each other. Right before arriving, he told me that he had just broken up with his girlfriend.

Nic picked me up from the Atlanta airport in his BMW—the same one Justin drove. A flash went through my mind of the last time I got into Justin's car when I had to break in to get my stuff he was holding hostage. *Whew, so glad I'm done with all that madness.*

Nic is a big, tall man with big energy, both powerful and childlike. My whole being lit up with excitement being around him. Our chemistry was magnetic and intense.

We went directly to R Thomas for lunch, sharing two raw food plates and a very stimulating conversation. That evening, I settled into the guest house on his multi-million-dollar property.

The next day, after our morning meeting, we walked a labyrinth in Grant Park and shared our insights. Things were happening fast, and it felt a little out of my control.

A few days into my stay, Nic confessed his strong attraction to me. We were both wrestling with giving in to it since I was working for him. I used my strong willpower and resisted.

I was standing in the guest house kitchen staring at Nic's text message, "I want you so bad."

I hesitated and then replied, "We can't," as my whole body got hot. I continued, "I need to keep our relationship professional."

It was impossible to resist our desires; our connection was too powerful for me to think clearly.

In an instant, my body changed my mind, and I went to his house. Nic was standing in the kitchen, and I could feel the heat between us as soon as I walked through the door. The way we kissed made me melt, and I thought, *Could he be the one?*

It had been seven years since I was in a relationship. Since I left Justin, I had focused my entire life on healing. *Maybe I am ready. Nic is different.* He's an extremely successful business consultant who's emotionally stable, creative, and intellectually stimulating. Nic tells me relationships aren't his thing. I think, *He probably just hasn't met his match yet.*

After leaving my business in Thailand, I needed to start over. Nic was excited to help me create a new business in Atlanta. I couldn't believe I landed there with someone so sexually and intellectually compatible who wanted to help me. *He must be the one.*

For two weeks, Nic and I spent the days brainstorming and whiteboarding, with some tantric time in the sheets. He paid me to complete a project with him that was due in one week, but he was also trying to convince me to stop the project and run off to the mountains together. I felt obligated to do what he paid me to do, so my *NO* was strong and firm with him.

That's when things flipped. Nic wasn't used to people, especially women, saying no to him. He always got what he wanted, so he completely closed off from me.

His silent anger was different from what I had experienced before. Nic withdrew his affection, saying, "We would never work out together; things are too complicated and intense."

I was devastated and extremely hurt, but I had to disconnect from my feelings to finish our project. It was good to have my old coping mechanisms in my back pocket when needed.

I thought Nic was going to help me make my dream a reality. Initially, he told me that after we were done with the project, he wanted to invest in a wellness center for me to run.

When I didn't run away to the mountains with him, Nic assured me, "I know one day you will be successful, Elicia."

I quickly replied, "I am already successful, Nic. I have done what most people, including yourself, will never do. I quit my corporate sales career, created my business, and sold everything I owned to live in Thailand, living from pure faith, inner guidance, and synchronicities."

Before I arrived, Nic told me I could stay in his guesthouse for two months. After only a few weeks, our personal and professional relationship ended abruptly.

He ran back to his "ex" and texted me, "Elicia, you need to leave immediately."

That night, I cried hysterically while trying to comfort myself with tequila and raw cacao.

With the little money I had left, I rented a house, trusting I could rebuild my business in Atlanta. Two weeks after moving out, Nic contacted me while I was at a 5Rhythms dance.

"I'm sorry," he said. "I was under a lot of pressure with our project and what others expected; that's what made me behave that way toward you. I was out of my mind. Please forgive me. I want to take you to dinner." Feeling both excited and guarded, I asked, "What about your girlfriend?"

Nic said, "We have an agreement; she knows I can't be with just one woman." What Nic wants, Nic gets.

I said, "I don't want to be with someone who is with someone else." But the pull toward him was overwhelming, drowning out my inner voice. Deep down, I knew I deserved a relationship with someone who was fully committed to me.

I tried to convince myself it was just casual, but the truth was I craved Nic's love desperately. My higher self was silenced by my wounded inner child's deep need for his affection.

I loved being taken out to nice dinners and sleeping at Nic's modern city penthouse. Whenever he wanted to see me, I would say yes. I was enjoying my freedom and having fun.

The first weekend I didn't have plans with anyone, Nic went away with his public girlfriend. She posted pictures of them together on Facebook. Seeing them felt like a dagger to my heart. The way she flaunted them together felt like a threat from her to me.

I felt the pain of not being with Nic and not being enough for him to choose me exclusively, so I sent him a text: "This is too hard for me. I don't want to see you again."

Silence. For a whole week, he didn't respond. Then, as if nothing had happened, he reached out, his words weaving a spell that pulled me back in.

I knew this wasn't right, but I agreed to dinner. The next morning, as he drove me home, a wave of nausea hit me. My nipples were tender. My period was late.

After seeing the double line pregnancy confirmation on the stick, I walked out my front door and lay down next to the angel statue on the grass to ground into this altering reality. Feeling supported by Mother Earth, I connected to my baby. A new love and purpose emerged.

I walked around the yellow house that I called *My Earth Goddess Home* to the backyard. The owners put so much love into this fairyland. I intentionally and slowly walked along the path, stopped at the Quan Yin statue and garden, and took a deep breath, taking in and feeling the nurturing divine love for me and my baby.

I knew Nic did not want a relationship, and he definitely did not want a child. So, I didn't expect him to be happy when I told him, but I also never imagined he would react the way he did.

I sent Nic a text message with a picture of the positive pregnancy test. No response, crickets. Then, I made it clearer and wrote, "I am pregnant."

Knowing this would create a huge problem in his relationship, I believe he started to go through the different stages of grief.

First, denial. Nic refused to believe I was pregnant. He demanded that I go to the doctor's office and get an "official test" to show him.

After I did that, he didn't believe the baby was his, even though he was the only one I was sleeping with. I was addicted to him; I don't think my body would have even been able to be with anyone else.

Then, he went into the second stage—anger. Nic thought I intentionally got pregnant to "trap him," even though I told him before the first time we had sex, "Please be careful, I'm not on the pill and I don't want to get pregnant." I flashed back to the moment he most likely forgot to pull out and denied it.

Once Nic got to the anger stage, he stayed there. His narcissism flared up, and he said some pretty nasty things to me, the woman who was carrying his baby.

He lashed out, blamed, and shunned me since it was going to come out that he got me pregnant. Nic shut me out of his life and hid behind his girlfriend.

The doctor visits were always stressful, the fetus wasn't growing, and there was a chance I was having a miscarriage. It was a lot to go through on my own.

During that period, Nic called me and confessed his love for me. One night, he wrote me a message, "Elicia, I know you are the one. I've just been too scared to open up to you in fear of losing myself to you."

I replied, "I will not be with you if you are still with her." The baby was helping me grow stronger.

After four long, stressful weeks of going to the doctor every week to check to see if the pregnancy was viable, it was confirmed that I had a miscarriage.

When I told Nic, he dropped everything, including his girlfriend, and told me he wanted to do it right this time with me. We attempted a relationship. He was still attached to his girlfriend and refused to take down a picture of her in his house, so we stayed at his city penthouse. I still didn't feel good enough for him.

Three weeks later, right before my birthday, Nic texted me to tell me we were over. I guess he felt guilty because he left me cash and a gift certificate to the spa we were supposed to go to together on my birthday.

Once again, I was left heartbroken, and his girlfriend took him back as usual. I was devastated and went into another dark depression. Still grieving the deep loss of my baby, I was also falling into a victimhood mindset.

Seeing someone in my network offer free intuitive readings on Facebook felt like a sign. I quickly booked a session and told her, "I want to be with Nic and have a baby with him. Why is this happening to me? Are we going to be together? I don't know what to do. Nothing is working in my life. I have no relationship or money, and now I have lost my baby, and I have a new strong longing for one."

Her voice was firm yet soothing. "Elicia," she said, "you need to have 'Fuck It Faith.' Faith that no matter what's happening—or not happening—right now, everything will work out. If you aren't with Nic and don't know how you'll make money, it will all fall into place with time and faith."

After the reading, I curled up in bed, picked up my journal, and wrote, "What brings me joy?" The answer flowed onto my page: "Teaching journaling workshops."

A spark ignited within me. Yes, this was the missing piece. I needed to reconnect with my heart's purpose and guide others to theirs. The memory of those workshops and the joy they brought flooded back. It didn't matter that they didn't bring in much money; they expanded my heart, which brought new opportunities.

I poured my energy into my journaling workshops and created customized programs for both groups and individuals. In addition to working with private clients, I taught marketing playshops for holistic practitioners in my living room.

My network and heart were expanding. I continued to share my teachings and insights on YouTube. Finally, after five long years of struggle and uncertainty, my business was supporting me financially.

I made a vision board with my dream life, including pictures of three men I cut out from magazines who emoted the qualities I desired in a man. One was mature, strong, and sexy, another was compassionate and good with kids, and another was totally into me, staring at me. I also pasted a wedding ring around me and my future husband on the vision board.

Nic came over once, saw my vision board, and even pointed out that he wasn't what I wanted. I would agree, flip-flop, and convince myself I might not want to be with one man.

Under my wounded spell, I even sent Nic an article about men who agreed to give women a baby but didn't have a relationship, thinking that's what I wanted.

I swore I would never be with him again. I knew he wasn't good for me. I knew what I wanted and what he wanted, and it didn't match. Whenever I tried to end it *for good*, Nic would tell me exactly what I wanted to hear.

> *I want to do a psychic reading with you to explore our past lives.*
> *Let's go shopping, my treat.*
> *I have reservations at this exclusive restaurant downtown.*
> *Here's a book to help you with your business model.*

I would feel weak, always wanting and needing what he had to offer. Each time I said yes, I felt rewarded because we had so much fun together. Just like any drug, I was on such a high when I was with him, and then I would crash and feel bad about myself when I wasn't with him. Nic held all the power, leaving me in constant anticipation, waiting for the next "hit" of connection.

I noticed a pattern: my client and money flow diminished when I was involved with him, even just wanting him. This created a cycle of dependence; I'd agree to dinners or business help, becoming a victim seeking a savior. However, when I found the strength to break away and reconnect with myself, I thrived.

The course leader's words, spoken during an intensive weekend workshop, echoed in my mind: "Your father is like cocaine to you. You're addicted to his love." Driven by a deeply buried longing for my father's love, I consistently chose men who reflected him, and Nic was just one example. Their emotional abandonment only deepened my yearning and perpetuated the cycle.

On one of our long breaks away from each other, I met a man, a kind and caring healer. He was very sweet and totally into me. Though happy with him, I still grieved the loss of my baby for months. This healer picked up that the spirit of the baby was still attached to me and suggested I see a shaman woman he knew in North Georgia.

Just as I began to fall for him, Nic sent me a message. I told him I had a boyfriend and asked him not to contact me again.

The next day, I received an email from Nic: *Elicia, I finally went to therapy like you suggested. I was talking about you and our baby, and I cried. I told my therapist I didn't know why I was crying, and he told me it's because I love you.*

He had never said the L word before, and again, I believed him. I hoped things would be different since he went to therapy.

The first weekend back together, I found out that my grandfather, whom I called Gramps, wasn't doing well. Gramps is one of my favorite people in the whole world, whom I love dearly. We had a very sweet and special relationship throughout my life. I felt truly loved and safe with him, so much so that as a preteen, I would fall asleep cuddling him.

At that moment, I was the only family member who could care for him. So I told Nic the first weekend we were back together that I had to drive down to Florida to take care of my Gramps, and he got upset with me.

A few months before I met the sweet healer man I briefly dated, I spent two months in Florida taking care of Gramps while I found him an in-home caretaker.

Each morning, we drew cards from my favorite TAO Oracle deck, and I would read them aloud. Gramps praised the strength and clarity of my voice.

He was a true champion of women; after retiring, he supported my grandmother's successful real estate career from its start in her fifties until her passing in her eighties. Together, they raised six remarkably independent, strong, and successful daughters.

One night during those two months with Gramps, I had a dream of a majestic white horse. The horse told me to climb onto its back, and together we galloped through a portal. I didn't know what it meant, but it felt positive and healing.

My mom and a few of her sisters came down to see their father and take care of some of his financial accounts. Upon returning from the bank, my mom surprised me with a small, stuffed white horse. "Ah, Portal Horse!" I exclaimed, recognizing the synchronicity and then sharing my dream with her.

When I received the call that Gramps had fired his caregiver and was struggling with basic tasks like putting on his pants, I didn't hesitate. The next day, I was on the road to Florida.

The following morning, Gramps drew the Deliverance card from the TAO Oracle deck.

Deliverance: "The time of Deliverance is captured best in the image of a thunderstorm. As in nature, when there has been a long dry spell, and thunderheads are gathering on the horizon, the time for deliverance is at hand. Before a storm breaks, the accumulation of energy and tension can build to a point where it feels almost unbearable. Then, the sudden release of pent-up energy in lightning and thunder delivers the earth from the oppressive conditions in the gusts of wind and cooling rains.

In the aftermath of all the storms and interplay of energies, in life, it is always important to maintain a spirit of open-heartedness and compassion. Forgiveness is a healing force, and it is just as important to forgive ourselves as it is to forgive others. In fact, the two often go together. By letting go of the past and its turmoil, you will clear the ground for the lessons of Deliverance to take firm root in the soil and grow into a deeper and more profound liberation of the spirit.

There is a window of opportunity now to move quickly and decisively into a new order of things, and this is best accomplished with heartfelt gratitude for all the lessons learned."

~ Ma Deva Padma

After dinner, Mom called to check in on Gramps. I stepped into the bedroom for a quick chat, but during our call, Gramps lost his balance and slipped, hitting his head on the wall. There was a bit of bleeding, but he seemed alright.

The next morning, I was surprised to find Gramps still in bed. He was usually up by four. I could hear him snoring, so I didn't disturb him.

However, by nine, a sense of unease crept in. I went to check on him and found him unresponsive with blood on his pillow. Panic surged through me as I frantically dialed 911.

At the emergency room, I learned the devastating news: Gramps, who was on blood thinners, had suffered internal bleeding in his brain overnight.

I spent three hours holding his soft yet strong tanned hand, as he held mine tightly. It was a precious and blessed time together to help him transition in peace.

I told him how much everyone loved him, how much I needed and cherished his love, that I wished to find a man like him, how Grammy was waiting to dance with him again in heaven, and what a meaningful life he lived. I thought about the Deliverance card he had pulled the day before and realized its profound meaning for him.

> *There is a window of opportunity now to move quickly and decisively into a new order of things, and this is best accomplished with heartfelt gratitude for all the lessons learned.*

Shortly after Gramp's funeral, I returned to Atlanta and went to a naturopath to treat H. pylori bacteria that did not go away with the water fast. I didn't say anything about my Gramps during my visit, but when I got home, I received an email from the office manager:

> *Elicia, you are always surrounded by angels. I saw them all around you. Your grandfather wanted me to tell you that he is very grateful for your presence*

and what you said to him when he was passing in the hospital. You helped him go without fear, and he loves you very much.

Shortly after that mystical message, I went to see the shaman in North Georgia. She helped remove the attachment to Gramps and my spirit baby so they could also move on.

Then, she told me something unexpected. She said: "There is a part of you waiting for you in the South of France, drinking wine on a balcony laughing her ass off. She's waiting for you to stop trying to make him understand."

I knew what she meant about "him," all the "hims" who don't understand me or themselves. I try and I try to get them to listen to me, but I end up drained and depleted, just like in my childhood. Living in the South of France didn't make sense, though; maybe she meant a past life waiting to integrate. I saved this in my heart.

I swore I couldn't go on like this with Nic anymore. All of our highs would crash and burn, and I would end up hurt and feeling alone.

When I returned from Florida, I went to Nic's city penthouse. While we were drinking sangria by the pool, I saw one of Justin's ex-girlfriends, who also lived with Will before I was with both of them. She was poolside with her husband and their newborn. A sign or a warning, perhaps?

Nic and I went up to his penthouse pretty buzzed. I looked at my phone and saw I had a missed call from Australia. I screamed, "Oh no," and broke down crying.

I had waited three weeks to have a session with the emotional therapist whom I last worked with in Thailand. Nic asked me what happened. While still crying, I told him I missed an important session I had scheduled with someone who lives in Australia because I got the time difference mixed up. Ironically, I booked this session because I felt desperate and conflicted because of my "relationship" with him.

That's when Nic yelled at me, "Stop crying and stop being such a VICTIM." His emotional abuse struck me hard, leaving me reeling. I grabbed my bag and fled.

Back in my apartment, I flung open the door and stumbled to the bathroom. Crumpled on the floor, my body shook uncontrollably, wailing and crying as I curled into a tight ball. I looked down and saw my stomach had grown as if I were six months pregnant. Yeast was pouring out into my underwear.

It was then, amidst the physical upheaval, that the truth hit me: my chronic symptoms were a manifestation of deep emotional pain.

For two weeks, I thought I could control it with the candida diet, again. Every morning, meditation and yoga. But that night, I knew. *No*, I thought, *it's not the diet, not parasites, not even my "perfect" spiritual practice.*

It's always been emotional.

I booked a session with my colleague, Janet, who confirmed what I suspected during an energy healing session. She said my inner child, who holds the power, was sitting Indian-style, knocking to come out.

Being with Nic triggered how my wounded inner child had felt with my dad: unlovable, not good enough, and emotionally abandoned.

I connected with my inner child using photos and my stuffed Portal Horse. I sat with her to express my anger and sadness about how I was treated as a child and how my childhood experience created the false belief that I was unlovable.

Every day, I looked at a picture of my two-year-old little girl (me) who felt ugly and unlovable. I told her I loved her and that she was perfect just the way she is, that she is special and lovable. I assured her that she deserves to be loved and cared for. I listened to how she felt about Nic and how much he hurt her.

A healer once said, "Every time you are with Nic, it's like throwing your inner child to the wolves." I fully felt and expressed my anger and sadness, and I stayed strong for her. I cuddled Portal Horse as my inner child and sent love from my heart to hers for all the times and ages she needed to feel loved.

I realized I had been overcompensating, striving for an unattainable "perfection" to mask a deep-seated shame. My restrictive eating habits, the never-ending pursuit to be skinny, and even my breast implants and long hair were all unconscious attempts to meet society's narrow beauty standards. Posting alluring photos on Facebook was my way of seeking external validation, while burying myself in work helped me feel needed and, therefore, worthy.

No diet, no spiritual practice, and no healer could fix what was hurting inside of me. The toxic patterns and the pain all stayed until I gave my inner child the emotional nurturance and support she longed for all along.

I felt and released emotions from the past triggered by Nic, and set strong boundaries to take care of my feelings. I stopped talking to him. I finally felt I deserved to be loved, cared for, and supported.

My physical symptoms vanished. The chronic yeast infections, the insatiable cravings, the emotional eating—all simply disappeared. I could eat freely without restriction or repercussions. I shifted my focus solely to my business and emotional well-being, letting go of the need to "fix" or help other practitioners. The compulsion to prove myself and seek external validation dissolved. In its place, a quiet confidence emerged. I am enough.

My inner child felt loved by me.

BIRTHDAY WISH

Since I became my own loving and emotionally nurturing parent, I didn't expect anyone else to take care of me and my emotional needs. After I finally, almost, shut the door on Nic, I met Dave, who loved me for me.

Dave gave my heart the experience I desired, to be loved for me, not my body or sex. We naturally went into pure presence with each other.

Shortly after meeting, Dave moved into my loft. Because he didn't have a car, I drove us everywhere. Before meeting me, Dave said he ate out for every meal, which was completely baffling since he was unemployed.

I ended up buying and cooking all our food, *and* I did the dishes. Meanwhile, Dave spent his time on my couch, working on an art program and not looking for a job. I was increasingly frustrated with the situation.

One day, I was cooking vegetable omelets in my open kitchen, while Dave was sitting on the couch on his computer. As I was cracking the eggs, I asked, "Dave, do you want to learn how to cook a meal just in case I get sick and can't cook?"

He quickly replied, "No."

At that point, I lost it and yelled, "You aren't making any money, you're not even trying to get a job, and you don't help out around the house at all. I'm so sick of taking care of you, and you don't even *want* to make an effort to help me." I was also angry at myself for allowing him to mooch off me.

Feeling proud of his meditation practice, while I was screaming at him, Dave said, "I love you, Elicia," and some bullshit like, "Your anger isn't mine."

The day before my thirty-ninth birthday, I was trying to decide if I wanted to break up with Dave before or after my birthday. I was sitting at my desk, the sun shining on my face through the walls of windows, and I proclaimed out loud, "I want someone who loves me for me AND who has their shit together. I'm going to get what I really want for my birthday." I broke up with Dave to make sure my wish came true.

On my birthday, I went out with my girlfriends to my favorite Mexican restaurant. When I was blowing out my candles, I thought, *I have everything I want except for one thing. I am ready for my soulmate.*

Later that night, when I got home, I opened Facebook and saw I had received a private message from someone named Doug. I didn't know Doug, but saw we were Facebook friends, although we had never interacted before.

Doug: *Is that guy in your pictures your boyfriend?*

Me: *Not anymore.*

Doug: *Coffee/lunch?*

Ugh, I thought. *I need a break from guys.* And I went to bed.

The next morning, I woke up to another message from Doug.

Doug: *Coffee/lunch?*

Me: *Okay.*

Being from New York, I liked both his directness and persistence, even though I found it slightly off that he didn't wish me a happy birthday. Doug tells everyone that he wanted to cut right to the chase. He didn't want to waste his time if I had a boyfriend.

We chatted on Messenger for a few days. Doug made me laugh by sharing big head emojis with silly captions. He was also very insightful. One of his gifts is that he can read photos. I said, "Go for it," and his description of who I am was pretty accurate.

Earlier that week, I updated my Facebook profile picture to one of my favorites from my time in Thailand. My mom came to visit me during my parents' divorce, and I surprised her with a night at Kamalaya, the five-star wellness retreat on Koh Samui.

She captured a photo of me in the pool, framed by columns and stone-carved goddesses. I mirrored their pose with prayer hands, my large breasts resting on top of the water matched their form, and my face radiated a similar serene expression. With my prayer hands, breasts, and arms reflected in the pool, I felt like the Goddess Aphrodite.

During this time in Thailand, I looked into removing my breast implants, but my medical intuitive told me that my body wasn't strong enough yet.

It turns out that in addition to my spiritual nature and other physical attributes, my double D breast implants were a big attraction for Doug when he first saw this photo.

As our conversation continued on Messenger, Doug asked me where I lived. I told him I was moving in a month and was currently looking for a place to rent in Kirkwood.

Pleasantly surprised, he told me he just bought a house in Kirkwood a year ago. Right away, Doug posted in the neighborhood groups to help me with my apartment search.

Our connection deepened when we discovered we had previously lived just around the corner from each other in Inman Park. That's when I lived in my favorite loft with my loverboy yellow lab, Hudson, before I moved to Thailand.

We even shared a niche culinary experience—we both ordered raw food delivery from the same couple at the same time, a memory that still made us cringe at the thought of the overpowering spices. It seemed Doug and I had a lot in common.

Having seen my Facebook photos, Doug thoughtfully suggested a Thai restaurant for our first date. When he greeted me, his intense blue eyes instantly captivated me. His gaze was so penetrating that it flustered me, and I stumbled over my words while trying to read the menu. "Um, ah, um, yeah ..." I stuttered.

Doug chuckled and said, "Oh good, it's not just me who feels that way." He went on to suggest that I'd probably never encountered a man in his own authentic power before. *Maybe not.*

Our conversation was exciting and stimulating. I thought how fun it was to be with a PhD psychologist, and I couldn't believe I hadn't considered that match before. What stimulates me the most is processing issues, seeing the cause, and making symbolic connections.

However, despite the instant deep connection, I told Doug that I wanted to take it slow. I had just come out of back-to-back relationships and needed some time alone.

As we left the restaurant, the afternoon sun still high, Doug suddenly smacked his lips against mine. Caught completely off guard, I blurted out, "Wow, you just went for it?!" He grinned, clearly pleased with himself.

That night, my earlier hesitations melted away in a wave of excitement. We talked for six exhilarating hours over the phone, delving into a connection I'd never experienced.

I loved talking with Doug; it was fun and interesting. I had never met a man who shared a similar intellect, intuition, and emotional connection as me before. Our shared enthusiasm led me to explore our astrological compatibility, and I read the entire twenty-page composite chart to him over the phone.

In essence, the stars foretold a union destined to heal our childhood emotional wounds and illuminate the path for others. Meeting Doug felt serendipitous, both magical and profoundly purposeful.

Before meeting Dave, a man asked me to come to his condo to watch a movie. He warned me, though, that his place was a total mess. So I turned him down.

My instant, deep connection with Doug helped me overlook the shocking disaster I walked into when I first went to his house. Although he had lived there for a year, it resembled a construction zone—boxes piled high, dog hair galore, and a layer of dust on every surface.

Doug proudly showed me around his house, pointing out the beautiful improvements he made, especially the unique granite countertops he selected. When we got to the sunroom, I noticed his elliptical machine and said, "This is my favorite for cardio."

He replied, "Well, good, because you can use it when you move in soon."

Taken aback, I said, "We'll see."

Within the first few days of our meeting, Doug was confident we would live together and marry. He seemed afraid and more possessive when I would say, "We'll see."

After five days, I knew I needed to break up with him because he was projecting onto me—men with mommy issues. I thought, *Great, here it is again; my purpose for meeting men is to send them to the course, the great course whisperer.*

On day six, we went to see the movie *Gravity*, a terrible choice in hindsight, considering the impending breakup. The film's relentless depiction of anxiety and fear in the vastness of space mirrored the tension between us.

Doug, sensing how I felt, kept glancing at me, searching for reassurance. His anxiousness only fueled my growing unease. My unspoken truth hung heavy in space, palpable to us both.

After our breakup, Doug was sad and had begun moving on, while I was drawn back into Nic's web of lies. Doug never left my mind. I found myself reaching out to check on him, which was confusing for him. I was just as confused; the desire to stay in touch with Doug was a new experience for me, especially considering our short-lived relationship.

Nic is back
Back again
Tell a friend
Shady's back
Shady's back
Shady's back.

Like having amnesia, I got together with Nic again, and he made his award-winning promises. I woke up Christmas morning full of anticipation for the day I had planned with him. Instead, I was greeted by a text: "Elicia, Merry Christmas and Happy New Year. I'll be out of the country until after the holidays."

I was furious and deflated. *WTF? Seriously? Again?* I thought to myself. Despite my anger at his lies and my gullibility, a part of me was relieved. Nic had shown his true colors once more, leaving no room for doubt.

As I looked around my apartment, my eyes fell on Dave's belongings. He was still lingering in my space. *Perfect timing,* I thought. *I'll return these today and finally close that chapter too.* This will be the last time I take care of Dave and his stuff.

I was dog-sitting Molly, my friend's adorable thirteen-year-old white fluffball. Molly was the perfect name for such a happy, loving dog. As I headed out to return Dave's belongings, I realized I would be passing Doug's street.

On a whim, I decided to call him. He answered, "Hi, Elicia."

I said, "Merry Christmas, Doug. What are you up to?"

He sounded surprised but happy to hear from me and replied, "Merry Christmas to you too, Elicia. Good timing—my kids just left. What are you up to?"

I asked, "Do you want to take Brocco for a walk with me and Molly on the Beltline?"

During our two-hour dog walk, while still infuriated, I told him all about the bullshit Nic had just put me through on Christmas morning. I shouted out loud with frustration a somewhat rhetorical question, "Errrrr, why do I go for assholes like Nic and push away nice guys like you?" Doug bit his tongue and said nothing.

The following week, Nic bombarded me with emails filled with lies. I finally reached my breaking point and told him, "I'm done, Nic. This is it. Don't contact me again."

That night, I shared an article on my Facebook wall titled "What Conscious Awake Women Want and Don't Want From Men." The article resonated with me, highlighting the common mistake of hoping emotionally stunted men will change and emphasizing the importance of choosing partners who are already emotionally evolved.

The following day, I mentioned to Doug that I was packing up to temporarily move in with a friend, as my Kirkwood apartment search was still unsuccessful. He immediately offered to help and arrived with a bottle of Don Julio Blanco, my favorite tequila, which was a thoughtful gesture.

I shook up two top-shelf margaritas, my signature drink, and we sat down before I continued to pack. Our conversation drifted toward the article I shared on Facebook. Doug secretly suspected it was a subtle message directed at him.

I reassured him, "You are the kind of man she is saying women want." Despite the undeniable connection, we settled into the friend zone, uncharted territory for both of us. Doug stayed the night, fully clothed. We slept next to each other in my bed, and like a gentleman, he kept his hands to himself.

We got up and moved my belongings to the house where I rented a room for January. My friends who owned the house were out of town for the holidays, so I was watching their dog, Molly.

It was New Year's Eve, and as I soaked in a hot Epsom salt bath infused with the essence of rose, champagne in hand, thoughts of Doug bubbled up. On a whim, I texted him.

Me: *Hey, what are you doing tonight?*

Doug: *Hey, good to hear from you. I'm going to my friend's party, which I go to every year. It's a fun NYE tradition. Lots of people, food, drinks, smoke, and live music. At midnight, we throw a vacuum cleaner off the balcony onto the grass.*

Me: *Sounds like fun.*

Doug: *Yeah, it will be. I'll be thinking about kissing you at midnight.*

Me: *Do you want to be thinking about it, or do you want to do it?*

Doug: *Huh? What?*

Me: *Can I come to the party with you?*

Doug: *Oh. Well, yeah, I guess so. What about Molly?*

Me: *I can bring her with me to your house and leave her with Brocco. They seemed to like each other on our walk.*

At the party, we mingled independently. I chatted and laughed with many new people I met that night. Doug, the performer, joined the band on harmonica. He even bravely sang a slightly off-key rendition of Jimi Hendrix's "All Along the Watchtower," which I found endearing.

As I stood against the wall, taking in the festivities, a wave of realization washed over me. Phrases I had said out loud to Doug, seemingly without conscious thought, echoed in my mind.

You are what women want.

Why do I push nice guys like you away?

At that moment, Doug did a drive-by, kissed me on the cheek, and said, "I love you, Elicia," and walked away.

Oh, IT'S HIM! Doug is my soulmate!

Our whirlwind romance was a testament to the unexpected. Doug and I met on my birthday on December 1, broke up six days later, walked our dogs together on Christmas, and fell in love on New Year's Eve.

As he predicted, I moved in immediately. Despite Doug already having two grown children, I was upfront about my desire for a baby. His love for me was so strong that he hesitantly agreed to embark on this journey.

While Doug was away at his course weekend, I tackled the daunting task of cleaning our house. I couldn't help but swear under my breath as I wiped the dust off his expensive stereo equipment.

But, even with the mess, I felt a surge of excitement for him. He was about to embark on the same transformative journey that had profoundly changed my life nine years earlier.

As the saying goes, *Build it, and they will come.* In Doug's case, it was more like *She will come, and then we'll get things done.*

Once I moved in, things started happening quickly. I thoroughly cleaned the house. Doug requested that his twenty-two-year-old son move out, and his room became my office.

Together, we spent the next three months renovating the master bathroom. Despite living and working together in the sunroom during the construction, our bond only grew stronger.

Our inner children were overjoyed. We finally got what we had craved our whole lives—our playfulness matched, we saw each other's gifts that nobody else did, and felt a deep, connected love. From this great container of love and support, our deepest wounds came up to be healed.

FROG CALL

An invitation to Frog Call Retreat in the North Georgia mountains arrived at the perfect moment. It was a gift from my dear friend Jimmie, whom I affectionately call J-Love. After two months of living in our sunroom while renovating the master bathroom, Doug and I were more than ready for a retreat in nature.

The intuitive who told me that I needed to have "Fuck It Faith" when I was falling apart after my miscarriage and heartbreak with Nic introduced Jimmie to me. She knew I could help Jimmie market her secluded getaway on 52 acres of private nature preserve in Dahlonega, Georgia.

Jimmie reached out to me, excited to share that she was opening her private family retreat to the public. She invited me for a tour of Frog Call, and I was equally excited to see it and get away from my stressful city life in Atlanta.

I was immediately enchanted as soon as I entered the long, winding driveway. A handcrafted wooden sign on a tree welcomed me: "Welcome to Frog Call, Seek Ye Peace in Nature!—J.C."

Jimmie greeted me with a warm smile and a hug. With genuine joy, she led me to the main cabin, which overlooked a tranquil pond with a small waterfall.

There were signs all around the beautiful, cozy cabin:

> *Love grows here.*
>
> *In every walk in nature, one receives far more than one seeks.*
>
> *I do yoga so I can stay flexible to kick my own arse if necessary.*
>
> *Love comforteth like sunshine after the rain.*

After the cabin tour, we walked down to the garden and across a charming bridge to a bunkhouse nestled away in the woods. We continued along the path to a long, custom-built bridge made of wood branches. It led over a hill and a freshwater creek, guiding us to a unique and inviting treehouse. As we explored the property's hiking trails, it was clear that this special place had been created with great love and intention.

I felt an instant connection with Jimmie. I opened up to her about the pain of my recent miscarriage with Nic and the weight of the responsibilities I was carrying for others.

Sensing my need for solitude and healing, Jimmie offered to let me stay the night at Frog Call by myself. That evening, I soaked in a soothing bath surrounded by beautiful natural stone tiles and walls of windows with a view of the tranquil pond.

At that moment, a wave of relief washed over me. Tears of gratitude welled up for this sanctuary and the kindness of my earth angel. What was meant to be a one-night stay turned into three days of healing and inner peace.

Later, as Jimmie and I discussed my experience, she suggested with a knowing smile that I would one day get married at Frog Call.

Within a few months, I was hosting private retreats for my clients at Frog Call and shared my photos on the newly created Facebook page. Jimmie, appreciating our connection and my help in launching and growing her business, would occasionally offer me complimentary stays during the week when there were no other guests.

One year after my initial visit, I received a special invitation: a romantic getaway for Doug, me, and our two dogs. Our first time together at Frog Call was magical. As we sat by the fireplace, our love sparked, mirroring the warmth of the crackling flames. Gazing into each other's eyes, we fell more deeply in love and knew we would get married.

The following morning, I received a text message from Nic: *Elicia, call me back, please. I miss you and want to see you.*

Despite my clear message to Nic that I had met my soulmate and wanted no further contact, he pursued me, disregarding my wishes.

I told Doug about Nic's messages, and Doug said he wanted to speak with Nic to make him stop disrespecting me and our relationship. We called Nic together, and he was stunned to hear from Doug.

Nic immediately asked, "Does Elicia know you are calling me?" After Doug told him I was sitting next to him, Nic asked to speak with me to confirm that was true. After I did, Doug firmly reiterated my desire for Nic to stop contacting me and to respect my boundaries.

We were both surprised when Nic admitted, "I guess I've been a jerk," to which Doug responded, "Yes, you have, Nic." I was deeply touched; no man had ever stood up for me like that before.

During the initial months of our relationship, unresolved issues around my body image and past objectification surfaced, demanding healing. In other words, I was easily triggered and often felt angry. The safe space of our loving, conscious relationship allowed these hidden wounds to emerge for true healing.

My insecurities flared when I mentioned wearing a size small shirt, and Doug innocently remarked that I couldn't possibly wear a small. In my mind, his words echoed those of my high school basketball coach, who had triggered my eating disorder with similar comments about my weight. I lashed out at Doug, accusing him of not understanding how to speak to women.

My slim figure suddenly gained a little extra weight when our relationship began, with no explanation or remedy. I sensed it was my soul's way of testing Doug's love, making sure it wasn't solely based on physical appearance, as had been the case with my past partners.

Despite my insecurities, I actually did wear a size small shirt, even at six feet tall with a larger bust. I was taller than Doug's previous partners, and he was a little shorter and smaller than me, which contributed to his misperception and comment.

During our second trip to Frog Call, we were sitting on the side of the hill looking at the treehouse when I broke down crying. Doug helped me explore the root of my body image struggles and persistent feelings of inadequacy. He guided me through an experiential therapy process, where I engaged in a dialogue with my grandmother and incorporated physical exercises to release deeply held emotions and beliefs.

Doug truly loved and supported me in so many ways I needed and longed for. In that moment of shared vulnerability, we discovered a mutual passion for experiential therapy, a field in which we both specialized.

Another challenge to my self-esteem and sense of security in our relationship was Doug's habit of openly admiring other women when we were together, despite otherwise supporting feminism.

After months of debating whether this behavior was appropriate, he finally agreed to see Dr. Mary with me. He defended himself by saying his previous partners had all accepted a "look but don't touch" policy.

It was deeply hurtful that the man I loved, who I believed was my soulmate, would think it was okay to ogle other women so blatantly. His knee-jerk reactions and commentary on women's appearances, even during movies or TV shows, left me feeling disrespected and insecure.

I first encountered Dr. Mary at the center where I had begun teaching journaling workshops again during the difficult period following my miscarriage and breakup with Nic. We called her Dr. because she was a Doctor of Chiropractic. For six months, I attended her workshops at the center and benefited greatly from her clear spiritual connection and clairvoyance.

During my first workshop, Dr. Mary intuited that I had been a twin in the womb, a possibility other intuitives had previously suggested. She explained that my twin had died very early in the pregnancy before anyone was aware of it, but that her soul had remained connected to mine.

According to Dr. Mary, this meant I had been carrying the karmic burden of two souls. While I couldn't say if this were true, it resonated with me. My life had certainly been filled with more than its share of challenges and difficulties up to that point. Yet I had no idea what was waiting.

Dr. Mary's approach was unique and empowering; instead of telling us what she knew, she would ask us questions to answer.

> *Who disconnects you from your power?*
> *Who keeps you from making money?*
> *Who prevents you from healing?*
> *Who is using you and draining your energy?*

Who is connected to your father wound?

The answer for me was always Nic. This became a running joke in the group; when participants were unsure about their answers, they'd simply respond "Nic," and we'd all laugh.

Back in the day, when Dave was mooching off me, I expressed my frustration that he was living with me without contributing anything. Dr. Mary responded with a smile and said, "He's perfect for you right now." Her cryptic message became clear to me: this situation was an opportunity for me to recognize my worth and establish healthy boundaries.

Dr. Mary's guidance was so impactful that I encouraged Doug to join me for couples counseling with her. Through our sessions, Doug began to understand the familiar and cultural origins of his behavior toward women. He expressed a genuine desire to evolve and create a more respectful dynamic between us.

After we completed our master bathroom renovation, we called it "The Spa." The large square room had a heated tile floor inspired by the tranquil master bath at Frog Call. My favorite was the jacuzzi tub for two, facing the walk-in shower covered with beautiful blue and gray tones of natural stone tiles and three burnt brass shower heads.

Even the modern waterfall faucets and natural stone sink bowls were inspired by Frog Call's lovely design. My closet was behind sliding mirror doors across from the bathtub and shower. The Spa was full of our love, reflecting the care and attention Doug and I poured into its creation.

Just as we were renovating our house, we were also renovating ourselves. Doug and I continued to navigate our intense emotional triggers together. Our first conscious relationship was a profound experience, with our projections and triggers serving as catalysts for deep healing and growth.

Our dynamic was complex: my attempts to offer Doug my support and understanding of some of his behaviors sometimes tapped into his feelings of shame and inadequacy, causing him to act defensively.

Seeing his reactions as defensiveness was a trigger for me. I would instinctively raise my voice to protect myself, and he responded with anger.

Feeling overwhelmed and unsafe, I would escape from the fight to create safety and lock myself in my office. Doug didn't understand my withdrawal, and it triggered his fear of abandonment, causing him to pursue me. He believed that he was just trying to discuss an issue.

In those episodes with Doug, I was transported back to my childhood home with my dad raging at my mom over nothing, me standing up to him for her, and nothing would help or make him stop.

I was in my childhood emotions, feeling unheard and deeply unsafe. I comforted my inner child and allowed all my feelings to be felt and expressed.

Once the storm had passed, Doug and I would reconnect, sharing our experiences and exploring the underlying triggers and unmet needs that had fueled the conflict.

Our unhealed wounds, like mirroring reflections, often collided and amplified each other, creating a minefield of emotional triggers.

Our enduring love, psychological skills, and insights provided a guiding light, illuminating the path toward healing and growth. Together, we were slowly learning to navigate the complexities of our relationship and pasts, one triggering moment at a time.

SUN DIAL

From the moment I felt my baby's presence, my longing to experience motherhood intensified. I shared this desire with Doug when we first met. The idea of having another child at fifty-two was daunting for him, especially with his two children already grown and newly independent. His willingness to embrace this life-changing decision at his age proved how much he truly loved me.

Five months into our relationship, I became pregnant, filling us both with immense joy. Embarking on motherhood later in life, after a long period of personal healing, I knew I was ready.

I ordered the best pregnancy books, kept a pregnancy journal, and knew what to eat and what supplements to take. I sought care from the same trusted midwife center where I went for my ultrasounds. Every step of the way, everything felt perfectly aligned.

Two weeks later, Doug booked a room for us at my favorite hotel, the Westin Downtown Atlanta, which has a breathtaking city view. I suspected he was going to propose there. One of the downsides of being so intuitive is that it's hard to be surprised.

Knowing I knew, he used his improv skills and suggested we visit BAPS, one of the most beautiful Indian Hindu temples in the US, before heading to the hotel.

The BAPS Shri Swaminarayan Mandir in Atlanta is a stunning white masterpiece of traditional Hindu architecture. We arrived and were instantly transported to the heart of ancient India. BAPS showcases itself on 30 acres of meticulously landscaped grounds, and there are over 34,000 hand-carved pieces of Italian marble, Turkish limestone, and Indian pink sandstone.

The air inside was infused with the fragrant aroma of incense, creating a sacred atmosphere. Flickering candles illuminated the Mandir and cast a warm glow on the intricate carvings, which created an atmosphere of reverence and tranquility.

I followed the rising smoke of the incense toward the heavens and imagined it carrying the prayers, chants, and devotion of the worshippers. When we arrived at the top floor, we were just in time for a candlelit ceremony, where men and women were seated separately. When it was over, I walked over to Doug, and he immediately dropped down to one knee, expressed his heartfelt love, and asked me to marry him.

Knowing I'd want to choose our wedding rings together, he had selected a temporary engagement ring with three meaningful stones, each representing our birth months—Doug's, mine, and our baby's.

When he pointed to the yellow stone, indicating it was for me, I was momentarily confused, as my birthstone is blue topaz. I asked him which month the stone symbolized, and he replied, "November because your birthday is November 30th, right?"

Very gently, I clarified that my birthday is actually December 1st. When I saw the mortified look on Doug's face, I sweetly embraced him and reassured him that it wasn't a big deal. It was a tender moment that allowed Doug to feel safe and accepted despite his slip-up. We've shared many laughs about the birthday stone confusion since that day.

Embracing and kissing, we felt a surge of love, connection, and commitment. At that moment, we found out that public displays of affection are not allowed in Hindu temples, so we were asked to stop and leave immediately.

We laughed hysterically all the way to our car—getting "kicked out" was our style anyway. We don't like strict rules, especially religious, and we are rebels. Before going to the hotel, we detoured home to relax, celebrate, and enjoy a swim in our pool.

After checking in, we ascended to the 73rd floor of the Westin Hotel to dine at the upscale Sun Dial Restaurant. Doug reserved a table against the floor-to-ceiling windows with a breathtaking panorama view of Atlanta.

As we gazed out at the sparkling city below, we toasted our engagement with glasses of champagne; I only had a celebratory sip since I was pregnant. At that moment, it felt like our dreams were coming true.

The time had come to share our news with Doug's children: we were engaged and expecting a baby. Doug had discussed our family plans with them early in our relationship, so they were somewhat prepared.

We invited them to dinner at our house on the pool deck. After enjoying raw zucchini "pasta" with Doug's homemade pesto, Doug announced that we had big news.

First, he shared our engagement, and they offered their congratulations, though their reactions were somewhat subdued. Then, he revealed the pregnancy. The news triggered a strong emotional response in both of his children. His son was wide-eyed, stunned into silence, while his daughter broke down crying hysterically. Doug tried to talk with them, but they were too overwhelmed to speak and left abruptly. We were blindsided by their intense reaction, and I felt devastated. Our joy and the love growing within me were met with unexpected rejection.

When I reflected on all these sudden changes—a stepmom and the prospect of another sibling—it must have been overwhelming. All of this also likely triggered unresolved emotions from their childhood experiences, especially their parents' divorce.

After the kids left, we struggled with their intense reaction to the pregnancy news. I urged Doug to talk to them individually to understand their feelings and concerns rather than making assumptions. He seemed reluctant and more comfortable taking the passive approach, hoping the situation would simply resolve with time.

His lack of initiative left me feeling isolated and unsupported in navigating this delicate and important family matter, and I'm sure his children felt the same. The baby in my belly became the elephant in the room. Integrating into an established family dynamic, especially as a disruptor, is difficult for everyone. I knew it would take a lot of work, time, and patience. So, I shifted my focus to the love Doug and I shared and the excitement of our upcoming wedding.

We wanted to get married sooner rather than later, plus we had to factor in my cousin's wedding that was coming up in October with my family's travel plans. We considered eloping, but I'd been there and done that, and it was important to us for our families to meet and celebrate together.

We chose the beginning of August, and as predicted, Jimmie generously offered our favorite place, Frog Call Retreat, as our wedding venue, making us the first couple to be married there.

With two months to plan, our wedding arrangements effortlessly fell into place. Jimmie recommended a gourmet caterer and a reception venue near Frog Call. I ordered my favorite flourless chocolate cake. With her natural gift for event planning, my mom offered her assistance every step of the way.

Fifty guests RSVP'd, and we chose the perfect outdoor spot behind the pond at Frog Call for our ceremony. We even hired an angelic woman to open our ceremony, playing crystal singing bowls. To make our day even more special, we asked Dr. Mary, who had helped us navigate our relationship challenges, to officiate our wedding.

One month before our wedding, we went for an ultrasound and received devastating news: I had miscarried. I went into shock and disbelief. This wasn't supposed to happen; everything felt so right—I was with my soulmate, and we were getting married.

I couldn't comprehend it. I spent the day grieving in our sunroom, and while Doug sat by me for a while, he was processing his own grief and took some space by running errands.

We called our closest friends and family to inform them of our loss, and we assured them that our wedding plans hadn't changed.

Shortly after my miscarriage, we flew up to Marshfield, Massachusetts, as planned, to spend a week at the beach with Doug's mom and meet his extended family before the wedding.

Still deep in grief, I mostly kept to myself as I sought comfort in reading books on his mom's couch to distract from my feelings. The love I felt for Doug and the excitement of our wedding kept me in my natural joy and high energy as we walked the beach each day.

HUMMINGBIRD

A week before the wedding, another serious fight raised my doubts about getting married. I went to Dr. Mary for some guidance.

Still reeling from the argument, I stormed into her office and blurted out, "I decided that I am not going to change my name to Miller, just in case it doesn't work out."

Dr. Mary helped me work through my doubts and see the bigger picture of our union. She encouraged me to change my name as a symbolic release of my old identity and a powerful step toward embracing our shared purpose. I would often joke that I went from a top-shelf bourbon, Woodford Reserve, to a cheap beer—it's Miller time.

August in Georgia isn't typically ideal for outdoor weddings due to the intense heat. A few days before the wedding, clouds covered the sky with rain, and I felt nature cooling the air. My earth angel, Jimmie, stepped in and set up a tent as a precaution.

On the morning of our wedding, I was gazing out the floor-to-ceiling bathroom windows, and saw the clouds clearing, mirroring the dissipation of my doubts.

As Doug got out of bed, I exclaimed, "The rain has stopped!"

With a grin, he replied, "Let's take a walk down to our wedding arch."

Doug held my hand as we strolled down to the pond. I was excited when a breathtaking sight greeted us: a pink lotus flower had bloomed, as if just for us.

Looking at Doug's joyful expression and sparkling eyes, a sense of profound assurance washed over me. Our union felt powerful, blessed by nature's gentle touch. The lotus, a symbol of growth and resilience in the midst of adversity, perfectly embodied the spirit of our love.

As I curled my hair, Mom joined me in the master bedroom for those essential pre-ceremony photos. She zipped up my dress as we looked at my reflection in the mirror, her eyes filled with love and happiness. She then handed me my beautiful bouquet.

My excitement grew as I dressed our dogs in their wedding attire: Brocco, our "best boy," in a dapper black tuxedo, and Molly, our "maid of honor," in a fluffy white tutu. *How perfect,* I thought, *to have our loyal, loving, and soul-connected companions by our side, supporting our love today.* Outside, Doug used his artistic touch to decorate our wedding arch with fresh flowers and greenery.

My friend, who had introduced me to the course a decade earlier, custom-designed our wedding rings. She envisioned a beautiful design with interlocking waves, symbolizing our union. The day Doug picked up our rose gold bands—mine adorned with small pink sapphires nestled along the waves—he surprised me with an additional matching band featuring a stunning, large pink sapphire for the crown. His thoughtfulness and constant surprises made me feel so loved.

As our fifty guests arrived, they were guided down the hill to gather near the pond, creating a natural aisle for us to walk through. My dad had healed, and our relationship was now loving and supportive. He greeted me with his teary, heartfelt eyes at the main cabin door to escort me down the aisle.

As I started to walk down the hill, Brocco ran up to me, proudly wearing his tuxedo, and took the lead, guiding us down the hill with his gentlemanly nature. *Good boy, Brocci.*

Brocco ran toward Doug, who was wiping the tears from his eyes. My dad hugged Doug as I embraced them both, and I kissed my dad on his cheek.

As I took Doug's hand, we paused and gazed deeply into each other's teary eyes, our love radiating through our smiles. Leading the way across the small bridge by the pond, the path opened onto a cozy, sun-sparkled clearing for our ceremony.

Chairs were arranged facing the flower-adorned arch, and Dr. Mary, our officiant, beamed a smile at us. Butterflies danced along the purple blooms that lined the arch and also fluttered in my stomach. The melodic sounds of angelic crystal singing bowls, nestled near the chairs, filled the air with a sense of peace as our guests took their seats.

I looked around and saw everyone smiling, and I locked eyes and hands with Doug. I felt the excitement from my inner child and the knowing of my higher self.

Dr. Mary commenced our wedding ceremony with a divinely beautiful invocation of love:

> *I'd like to welcome you all on August 2nd to the marriage ceremony of Douglas Jay Miller and Elicia Marie Woodford.*
>
> *I've had the pleasure of knowing both of them deeply and could not find a better match on this planet set up by God so that both individuals will be able to grow into the people that God set for them on their life's journey.*
>
> *Love is not about kindness. It's about being kind even when you don't want to. Love is not about passion. It's about being passionate when everything looks dull. Life is not about forgiveness. It's about forgiving yourself and others as soon as possible when a problem arises so that you may return to the complete connection in God's holy name.*
>
> *Let's be clear that love is God, and you are God's holy creatures filled with a capacity of love that can only be reached when you're together. Thank God often. When there is union created as the union created by these two people, the world benefits.*

Following Dr. Mary's beautiful and clear message about love and our divine union, my dear friend Evelyn, a kindred spirit with profound spiritual depth and loving kindness, shared her insights on love.

> *Love, what a beautiful subject to contemplate. Spiritual leaders have said that love is a dynamic, inspiring throbbing of the heart. Love is our only reason for living and the only purpose of life. We live for the sake of life, and we live seeking love. Everything we do in life, we do in hopes of experiencing love. Not surprisingly, we keep looking for love because we are born of love, and we come out of love. We are all vibrational creatures of love. We are sustained by love, and in the end, we merge with love.*

Evelyn continued, offering her heartfelt sentiments and blessings for our union:

> *Elicia and Doug, thank you for inviting us to this experience of love. In your presence, love is so palpable. In your presence, I feel giddy and joyful, engaged and inspired. Your commitment to each other is evident in the way that you so willingly step into the challenging moments in any relationship that serve as the gateway to a deeper experience of love. Your courage and commitment are inspiring to me, and I'm sure it's safe to say to us all.*

Everyone appreciated Evelyn's sweet expressions of love. Dr. Mary continued, "This relationship is about growth. These two are on the fast track to growth in this life experience." This truth was felt deeply in my body.

Dr. Mary then presented the Native American wedding vase, explaining its symbolism: "Drinking from one vase but from separated spouts signifies that you are both individuals, yet united by this shared vessel."

As I drank, a bit of water spilled down my chin, and I let out a surprised giggle.

Doug joked, "Here, let me get that for you!"

Dr. Mary playfully tapped his arm and said, "Shh, not now!"

After swallowing, I said, "That was on purpose—it went straight to my heart."

With a shared chuckle, Doug took his drink, and Dr. Mary invited him to begin the vows.

>Doug:
>
>*Elicia, you are so beautiful, and your eyes are always wonderful to look into. This began through an effortless act with intent that is seen as an act of grace guided by love, guiding our love. We both were enchanted, literally speechless, when we met. An omen of what is here now.*
>
>*A deep and profound sacred union for both of us, full and fulfilling. You are the key to my Soul's Renaissance. You have awakened me in the deepest way that I have ever experienced. You are my mate, my match, and beyond. You bring out the best of me to embrace life and the mystery.*

My deepest goal is to love well, and you allow me to fulfill that goal. You are my divine feminine, a beautiful mystery, always exciting and new. You'll always captivate my attention.

There was a time in my life when a song would go through my head—"I Need a Miracle" by the Grateful Dead. Truly, every day is a miracle one way or another with you. Your vulnerability is most precious and dear to me. I promise to meet yours with my own.

I love you with all my heart. I vow to remain loyal to you in all ways, honor you, and hold you in esteem at all times.

As I listened to Doug's vows, tears welled up in my eyes, and love radiated from my heart. His deep, resonant voice washed over me, and I absorbed his heartfelt words completely.

Elicia:

Doug, thank God that I met you. I love you so much. I love your bright light and your playful joy and your big, wide-open heart. I dreamed of you, I wrote about you. I plastered you all over vision boards, and I held you close to my heart with faith, and after thirty-nine years, you came to me on my birthday, the greatest gift of all.

You are more than the fifty things I wrote on my list. I had no idea how it would feel; I hoped that it

> would be something different than I've ever known, and it is.
>
> I have a whole list of things that you are that I love about you. I'll just read the top ones: loving, caring, and so supportive, you really support me, and that is transforming my life.
>
> Besides being super smart, you're also sexy and goofy—and goofy was at the top of my list. (Our guests chuckled as I gave Doug a big, playful smile.)
>
> Humor is the most important thing, to laugh and play all day with the animals. You're so nurturing, I think you're even more nurturing than me. It's beautiful for you to show other men how to be nurturing, supportive, sensitive, and caring. I'm proud to be with you. You're so strong, you can handle me, and it's a lot to handle.

Doug then gestured with his hand that he kind of could, while I nodded more and more that I was a lot, and we all laughed.

> You are very handsome, playful, super aware—you meet me. You are innovative and so handy, Mr. Fix-It. I love living with you, and I love how you take care of everything, and that is transforming my life. You are creative, compassionate, a lifesaver, and a changer in so many people's lives. Most of all, you meet me in the depths of my soul.
>
> I feel your love when I look into your gorgeous eyes. I feel your love when I hear your penetrating voice. I

feel your love when we are laughing. I feel your love when you support and take care of me. I truly feel loved and cared for, and that is transforming my life.

We were made for each other. We have a solid devotion to each other, our relationship, our family, and our individual growth. We create a safe space to be vulnerable, free, goofy, and grow.

I promise to help you love life.

At that moment, a hummingbird flew down the aisle and hovered above Doug's head while everyone gasped, except us, since we didn't know that happened until afterward when people told us.

I will always hold you with tenderness, and have the patience that love demands to live within the warmth of your heart and call it home, today and always. I need you beside me, as my best friend, lover, and forever soulmate. I love you, Douglas Jay Miller.

My friend Shereen then presented us with the rings.

Dr. Mary asked Doug, "Do you take Elicia to be your wife, to be everything and nothing when the time is needed to be her rock, her lover?"

Our little white fluff ball dog Molly rolled on the grass in her little tutu in front of Doug while Dr. Mary continued, "To be that which God trusts you to help you and Elicia through the harsh times, through the hardest times, through those times God has set for only the two of you to share?"

Doug replied, "Absolutely and totally," as he put the rings on my finger and kissed my hand.

Dr. Mary continued, "Elicia, do you take Doug as your husband, a friend, a confidant, and a mystery that will constantly unfold as you age together in perfect union?"

I replied, "Absolutely and totally, I do." I put the ring on Doug's finger and kissed his hand.

Dr. Mary proclaimed, "As God is our witness, I now pronounce you man and wife. Doug, you may kiss the bride."

Doug dipped me into a passionate kiss as our guests erupted in cheers. Everything felt perfect.

Dr. Mary announced, "I'd like to be the first to introduce Doug and Elicia Miller." Brocco, in his role as "best boy," greeted each person sitting along the aisle.

My Dad blurted out to Doug, "Now you are responsible."

I replied, "I am very capable."

Brocco then blessed us by walking through us.

Walking down the aisle, a wave of pure joy ran through my body. I whispered to Doug, "Should we skip?" He laughed and held my hand as we skipped like children, Brocco trotting happily beside us.

Dr. Mary greeted us with a warm kiss and heartfelt congratulations. We paused by the pond, basking in the love and happiness radiating from our guests as they crossed the bridge to embrace us.

After a joyous reception, I cuddled up to Doug on a couch on the screened-in porch of the main cabin, the tranquil pond shimmering below. I felt completely satiated—the catered buffet had been exceptional, especially the divine flourless chocolate cake.

Following our first dance to "Lovesong" by The Cure, played by my brother, the DJ, the dance floor erupted with a playlist of all my favorite songs. I felt pure joy, my feet barely touching the ground, and my heart expanded.

Doug shared that our ceremony had profoundly shifted something within him. He felt more secure within our relationship, and any lingering anxieties or uncertainties had vanished. I, too, felt a similar shift—a deepening of our bond, a renewed spark of love and attraction.

Back home, I eagerly awaited the arrival of our wedding video from our videographer.

"Honey, let's watch our wedding video!" I called out to Doug excitedly. Curled up in bed with coffee, I inserted the DVD into my computer. As we relived the ceremony, the profound truth in Dr. Mary's words, Evelyn's insights, and our vows resonated deeply, bringing tears to our eyes.

We rewound and replayed the moment in my vows where I promised to help Doug love life, finally witnessing the hummingbird that had gracefully flown down the aisle and hovered above his head.

Soon after, we were completely blown away when we saw a detail we had missed on our wedding day: a hummingbird tattoo on Dr. Mary's back. From that day on, hummingbirds became a special symbol of love, appearing in significant moments.

After our ceremony, our videographer had Doug's friend, John, interview our family and friends, capturing heartwarming and entertaining interviews.

Some things were said over and over by our family and friends:

"The hummingbird was very auspicious."

"Their love sprang forth a desire within me for a loving relationship."

"The setting is perfect for them; everything feels just right."

"I'm so happy that they found each other."

What especially moved me was when my mom said this about me ...

"Elicia has so many layers to her, and she's so full of life. She looks to meet and greet people. She has a lot of love in her. I'm so glad she met Doug because she had all this love building and building in her until it was just gonna explode, and she's able to do that with him. I'm just very happy for her because she's a multifaceted, lovely living being, and I love her very much."

Hearing my mom's unexpected praise caught me off guard; at the time, my emotional wounds prevented me from appreciating her words. Now, after fully healing my mother wound, I understand she truly saw me, even if she struggled to express it throughout my life.

John: *She is full of life. I remember when I first met her, I thought, wow, there's something large about her, multifaceted doesn't even cover it. I think the best is yet to come. There's more to be uncovered.*

Mom: *She comes from good stock. My parents were amazing people, and she saw them with a rich environment full of love and dance, lots of dance and good times. So she's become this person who just wants to experience everything. She actually inspires me because I love to live life, but I don't have the energy she does, but she's just really who anybody would want to be to experience life.*

John: *I think as a person, and I look at her even as a gay man, I want my partner to be like this woman who's just full of life and nurturance, and who will stand guard with the things that I want in my life.*

Kathy, Crystal Singing Bowls: *It's the kind of heart-opening experience that makes you want to turn to the person next to you and appreciate the heart in them. They're the kind of example of the couple that we want to grow toward. It just feels really good to be around them for who they are as individuals, but when they come together, it just amplifies that heart sense and heart energy, and I'm so grateful to be here today. It was just a beautiful experience.*

Everyone's beautiful descriptions deeply moved us, and heartfelt feelings were shared about us, our wedding, and our relationship. What a blessing to start our new lives together. With so much love circling us, a new chapter was waiting with many gifts to unwrap.

SPIRIT BABIES

I was consumed by a powerful urge to create both a baby and my new business, and it felt exhilarating. Doug, one of the top forensic psychologists in Georgia, was busy with his evaluations, but we still found time each afternoon to walk Brocco and Molly through the Kirkwood Urban Forest right across the street from our house.

These walks often extended through the neighborhood to a casual dinner in town, where we would discuss our work and delve into deeper topics. Sharing this passion energized us and also nurtured a sense of connection, understanding, and support, fulfilling our long-held needs.

When I legally changed my name, I rebranded as EliciaMiller.com with the tagline "Your Symptoms Are a Gift," a concept that resonated deeply with me.

When Doug inquired, I shared that my symptoms had been a doorway to understanding emotional root causes and the need for deeper healing, a process I guide clients through. I shared an example of the link between candida and codependency, and how symptoms hold specific messages.

Doug presented me with a very thick book he had received years earlier, *Messages from the Body*, which perfectly aligned with my approach. This synchronicity surprised both of us, as life gave us a wink.

For the past decade, the ebook by Michael J. Lincoln, PhD, has become an invaluable resource for my clients, affectionately named by many of them as "The Bible."

Coinciding with the launch of my new business, I thought I was pregnant. My desire to be pregnant was so strong that my body would manifest pregnancy symptoms even when I wasn't actually pregnant.

This became a recurring cycle of hope and disappointment: I'd experience tender breasts and a bloated belly, take a pregnancy test, and feel let down looking at the negative result.

Doug's internal conflict about starting over with a child was clear. He felt mixed emotions after our first miscarriage—sadness and relief. Each pregnancy brought him joy, but also worry.

He tried to express the challenges and life changes of raising a child, but my overwhelming desire to have a baby drowned out his concerns. And the unspoken disapproval of Doug's young adult children cast a shadow over my joy. Doug still didn't want to rock the boat with them, and we all felt unsupported.

After our second, my third, heartbreaking miscarriage, I sought answers from my intuitive team. An energy healer offered reassurance that things would eventually fall into place.

My medical intuitive suggested a karmic incompatibility with the specific soul, and we invoked a more harmonious one. A spiritual teacher said that if God intended for me to have a child, it would happen.

Seeking further insight, I booked an Akashic Records reading. Without knowing my history, she revealed past-life karma with me, Doug, and children. She said that to resolve the karma, as an advanced soul, I contracted with souls who desired to experience 3D life but who did not want to be born.

To explore every possibility, I also consulted my OB-GYN and underwent testing. The test came back positive for Factor V Leiden, the blood-clotting gene. We figured that was why I was losing my pregnancies. As soon as I found out I was pregnant again, I reluctantly shot up every day with a blood thinner, Lovenox.

I went for an ultrasound at the midwife center where I had been going each time since my first pregnancy with Nic. When the doctor saw me walk through the door, he looked surprised to see me again. There seemed to be something he knew that I didn't know about my pregnancy path. His look stayed with me.

A few weeks later, it was confirmed that I miscarried. Deep grief became my friend. I was as determined to find the cause of my miscarriages as I was with my candida symptoms. *There must be a reason I felt this strong desire for a baby.*

After our third miscarriage, I consulted a naturopath who specialized in pregnancy. She promised me her program and supplements would lead to a successful pregnancy. When I returned home and told Doug what she had said, he was very skeptical and asked, "How can anyone guarantee such an outcome?"

My blood work revealed depleted hormones, so the naturopath prescribed supplements to replenish my vitamin D, B vitamins, iron, and progesterone for two months.

We conceived again, and this time, we were very hopeful. Right after seeing the heartbeat, we lost our baby at nine weeks. As we were grieving, Doug discovered a dead baby hummingbird behind the chaise lounge where I often worked. We interpreted it as a loving message from our lost child.

After our fourth, my fifth, heartbreaking miscarriage, I detached from tests and the desire to have a baby. I just connected to the soul. I opted out of a trip to see Doug's family up north and stayed home alone to read the book *Spirit Babies: How to Communicate with the Child You're Meant to Have* by clairvoyant and medium Walter Makichen. This book gave me great comfort. I read it in our sunroom recliner, absorbed in the channeled messages about miscarriages and their meanings. I was touched by the sweet stories, and the sight of the single rose beside my Tara statue on the table in front of me connected me to a sense of peace.

A few months later, I was sitting in our sunroom, and an insight came to me about my breast implants. During the naturopathic exam, she inquired about my breast implants, but she didn't raise any concerns, even though I had some unusual symptoms, like excessive earwax, which she removed with a machine.

Something about that experience felt off, so I researched the potential link between my symptoms and breast implants. It was a revelation. My compromised immune system, likely due to the implants, explained my earwax, leg pain, swollen lymph nodes, and breast pain. It also dawned on me that this could be the cause of my miscarriages.

My online research led me to Dr. Susan Kolb, author of *The Naked Truth About Breast Implants*, whose practice was conveniently located in Atlanta.

I immediately decided to schedule an explant surgery. I tend to make swift decisions, sometimes without considering the impact on others. I rushed to tell Doug about my decision.

His initial reaction, focused on his preference for my appearance, triggered my frustration at feeling unsupported, leading to an argument. The next day, after cooling down, we had a productive conversation where we both felt heard and understood.

Doug and I visited Dr. Kolb together. After an examination and ultrasound on my armpits, she explained that silicone had leaked into my lymph nodes. The surgery would be complex, involving the removal of the implants, affected lymph nodes, and any residual silicone. She would also perform a breast lift to address the stretched skin.

Dr. Kolb offered a comprehensive approach to restoring my health through her expertise in explant surgery and holistic health practices, including detoxification protocols. We left feeling optimistic and hopeful about the journey ahead. This would be my final detox.

Dr. Kolb and her colleague, another skilled plastic surgeon, collaborated on my surgery, which lasted eight hours under anesthesia. Awakening the next day, I experienced a profound sense of self-connection and an overwhelming wave of unconditional self-love. It felt as though the implants had masked not only my physical body but also my emotional core and capacity for empathy. My body and soul felt stronger and lighter.

MOTHER'S MILK

Six weeks following my explant surgery, I reconnected with Veenaa, the shamanic healer from my time in San Francisco, to request a reading.

I wanted to know:

- What my body needed to heal from the operation and breast implants
- What was causing constipation, swollen glands, and clogged ears
- If my body was ready for pregnancy

I found out through the reading that everything was lined up perfectly for me to remove my breast implants and clear the toxins from my body for a higher level of vibration for me and a baby. It was an important time for me; going through a heart upgrade with more nurturance for my breasts and mother's milk.

Veenaa saw two inflamed spots around my ovaries, and my second chakra had some blocks from the past. My reproductive organs were inflamed. Deep energy healing work was necessary and due. A clearing was also needed all down my legs because there had been some tension in the past about moving forward with starting a family and my work.

Veenaa also saw an old psychic cord wrapped around my throat that needed to be cleared because it was preventing me from speaking my truth clearly. Hormones were being produced that were stress-based; tension and worry were affecting my immune system, health, and vitality. This was a result of trauma during childhood.

My mind was seeing things as dangerous, causing a stress-based chemical soup that contributed to losing my pregnancies. I feared danger because my needs were not being provided for, and people's behavior around me was triggering tension.

The silicone was adding to all that, secreting toxins that were mixing with the chemicals. I had cleared 30-40%, and I needed to clear a lot more to bring myself into full alignment with the true source of who I am.

I also needed to step back from any strong desire to have a child. I was going through a massive upgrade and needed to treat myself as a child. She suggested we wait another six months because any trauma I had at birth would get activated if I got pregnant.

I booked a shamanic psychic surgery session the next day to clear what was needed. To prepare, I smudged my office with incense and lit candles. I lay on the bed beside my desk, covered by a soft white down comforter.

Veenaa began the Skype session and helped me quiet my mind with guided deep breathing. Light sparkled on me from the window. She led me into a shamanic journey with rhythmic drumming, and I was instantly transported. I felt white light and a divine presence around me.

During the two-hour shamanic journey, we cleared a subconscious fear rooted in my childhood: the fear of not measuring up in my relationships, of not being loved or provided for.

She also cleared old hurts from past relationships in my heart. I let out a powerful vocalization, releasing what had been held tight in my throat. Veenaa did a lot of clearing in my head and legs, and through soul retrieval, I brought in more self-love and abundance.

Following the session, I gained a deeper understanding of the emotional healing process for candida. It became clear that it originates from a fear or belief that one's emotional needs will not be met, often rooted in childhood experiences where those needs were neglected.

Veenaa gifted me her book, *The Magdalene Letters: Flame of Ascension*. She wrote a collection of channeled letters addressing themes significant to Magdalene: justice, sexuality and gender, women's equality and empowerment, human rights, and the truth around Yeshua and the priestesshood.

She channeled sacred codes and embedded them in the book to empower anyone who either read or even came into contact with the book. I absorbed the book in one day, deeply feeling the embodied truth and empowerment.

After seven months dedicated to physical and emotional healing, during which I intentionally set aside thoughts of pregnancy, I felt balanced and whole.

When I discovered a ten-week fertility visualization program, I signed up immediately, and I soon became pregnant. The signs were abundant, and I felt hopeful, relaxed, and confident. At our eight-week ultrasound, we were overjoyed to hear a heartbeat.

My joy was once again overshadowed by the ongoing tension with Doug's daughter, who stopped talking to him due to our fifth pregnancy and her mother's influence.

My attempt to ease the situation by texting her about his birthday dinner backfired, as she told me to stay out of it, leaving me feeling hurt and excluded.

Doug's son came over before we left for dinner. While we were standing in the kitchen, he looked down at our ultrasound on the granite, and we felt his happiness for us and his future brother. When Doug's daughter arrived with her boyfriend, she shifted the focus, and we were left feeling hurt and ignored on Doug's birthday.

The following week, I had a nonstop headache for three days, so we went for an ultrasound. Just as my ten-week program ended, so did my pregnancy. When we found out it wasn't moving forward, I started to cry, and my headache went away.

The bleeding started as soon as we got home. That night, intense cramps woke me at two in the morning. I sat on the toilet, moaning in agony. Doug found me curled up on the bathroom floor, crying, and helped me back to bed.

Minutes later, I ran back to the bathroom, screaming and biting my tongue, gripping the toilet in pain as I fell to the floor. Doug stayed by my side through it all, comforting me as best he could.

For the next couple of hours, I endured intense cramping, contractions, and chills. The pain was so unbearable that at one point I nearly vomited and passed out at the same time. My body was releasing in a powerfully primal way.

The pain of miscarriage is often worse than labor because the cervix isn't thinned and ready to open. Doug took care of me, held me, and found pain medication that made it bearable.

This all happened on the cusp of the new moon in Gemini, during the Grand Cross. I came across this channeled message from astrologer Sarah Varcas that perfectly described my miscarriage experience, and resonated in my heart.

> "This New Moon nourishes our inherent bodily wisdom that simply knows the truth beyond explanations, theories, and words.
>
> We may want to think our way through it, but right now it is time to feel as well, to allow our bodies to speak and a felt sense of deep knowing to arise. Therein lies all the wisdom and advice we will need."

I had a spontaneous miscarriage, and my body released everything on its own. *It was the most painful experience of my life.*

Before the physical release, I questioned if having a baby was meant to be, filled with resistance and the fear of another loss. Following the release, my mind found stillness, and my questions and fear vanished. I felt a deep sense of peace, love, and hope that transcended the earthly realm.

With every other miscarriage, I had undergone a D&C operation, and never truly felt the loss in my body. Unconscious during the procedure, I had no memory of the baby leaving me, which only intensified my grief afterward. *Something crucial had been missing: the profound experience of feeling the physical pain.*

Consciously experiencing the physical and emotional loss brought a sense of completeness and renewal. I also realized that my connection with my angel babies deepened my ability to guide clients with their inner child healing. I don't feel a loss; I know they are with me.

As a part of my grieving process, I felt the need to share my loss on Facebook, which I had been reluctant to do in the past. Miscarriages are not talked about much, in part because there has been shame associated with too many questions from others suggesting that something is wrong with you.

The night we found out, I posted a picture of a woman holding an angel baby with the caption, "My sixth angel baby left us today at eight weeks pregnant. #grieving."

It was incredibly healing to receive so much love and support through that post. Three hundred people commented on that post, and I received many private messages and emails of hope, love, and offerings.

Doug also posted a long article in a men's group he started on Facebook. He received great support regarding his journey of starting a second family and enduring these repeated losses.

People I hadn't spoken with in decades wrote to me to share their story. Many said they see the divine love between us and already perceive us as conscious parents.

Our vulnerability and openness led to an outpouring of love and support and helped us navigate our grief. Feeling less alone in our pain, I was also empowered to set boundaries with those who tried to offer unsolicited advice or judgment. The water fast leader jumped in, posting that I should have stuck to the all-fruit diet. I immediately blocked him.

I realized the pregnancy journey is very much like the healing journey.

The same principles that helped me while I was healing from candida and addictive patterns—the ones I teach my clients—apply:

Keep the faith.

Visualize and believe.

Feel your emotions.

Be vulnerable and open.

Ask for and receive support.

Surrender to the journey.

You are not in control of when it happens.

Don't give up when there are setbacks.

Keep exploring potential causes.
This is your path; avoid comparisons.
Everything will align in the right time.
Trust in the process.

THE SEED

I hosted my first emotional healing retreat with my friend and retreat partner, Janet, in the beautiful beach town of Santa Teresa, Costa Rica. After flying from Atlanta to San Jose, we met our retreat group at a bed and breakfast for an overnight stay.

Early the next morning, we embarked on a fun van journey to the ferry. On the ferry's upper deck, the group took in the stunning views, snapped selfies, and enjoyed the warm tropical sun and ocean breeze.

Excitement was rippling through us as we neared our destination at the tip of the Nicoya Peninsula. When we arrived at the dock, we continued in the van, eventually reaching our private retreat center in Santa Teresa.

In those days, the town was so wonderfully *tranquilo*. The jungle extended to the expansive beach with perfect surfing waves and breathtaking sunsets.

Doug joined the retreat in a supportive role, offering individual dream interpretations during meals and remaining present outside the group sessions.

Each morning, we gathered for a private yoga session and enjoyed three delicious, healthy meals together. My mouth waters thinking about that falafel sandwich with hummus.

In our private villa, I shared the process coming through me—the sequence, the teachings, and the experiential exercises. Doug recognized that a potent psychological and emotional healing model was emerging, and he was very excited about it.

During the retreat, I saw how quickly people could access and express their repressed emotions through the process and within the group.

One night, as the group members were releasing their repressed anger in their villas, the sky erupted into one of the most intense thunderstorms I had ever heard or felt.

Marveling at the storm's intensity, Doug turned to Janet and asked, "Is the sky closer?"

Janet shot back a playful, "Yeah, Doug, the sky's closer," and we all burst into laughter.

That night during the storm, I dreamt of each person. One by one, their faces rose from my stomach to my head. I intuitively understood their childhood feelings and needs.

Doug, awake and observing me, described my process as profoundly shamanic—he even saw smoke rising from my belly and leaving through the ceiling.

The next morning, when we gathered for our first session, the entire group felt lighter. After hearing about their new shifts and insights, we walked to the beach and swam in the ocean for a ceremonial cleanse.

I felt a deep connection to both the land and the emotional world of each person. In the group sessions,

I intuitively knew where they needed to go emotionally and how to guide them gently past their defenses.

As the week progressed, the women began eating less at meals, feeling nourished through emotionally supporting their inner children. In one session, I sat beside a woman, placing a comforting hand on her back, and guided her to the moment her inner child learned to use illness to gain support. I helped her reconnect with those feelings and give her inner child the true support she craved.

The reconnection and release of repressed emotions unleashed her intuitive gifts, and she started to channel messages for others. At the end of the retreat, she shared a message with me that resonated deeply: "Elicia, you are powerful, and your empathy will continue to grow."

Each woman experienced significant shifts afterward: they let go of dysfunctional relationships and were more nurturing with their bodies and emotions. However, it became clear that they needed more time to prepare for the process, slowing down the pace to allow for deeper and ongoing emotional release and support as the healing process unfolds. One week was just the starting point.

The retreat was transformative for me as well. It reshaped my approach to private client work and revealed the power and importance of deep emotional work within a group setting. Santa Teresa also planted a seed in Doug and me.

Janet and I ultimately discovered the ideal location for our biannual Sacred Emotion Retreat: The Retreat Costa Rica, Wellness Resort and Spa, nestled atop a crystal-quartz mountain with breathtaking vistas of the canyon forest and ocean. The gourmet raw food chefs prepared exquisite, nourishing farm-to-table meals, and they quickly became our close friends.

Every aspect of The Retreat was perfectly suited to our group's needs, from the luxurious accommodations and serene yoga studio to the rejuvenating spa and inviting restaurant with a salt water pool sunset view. All this was complemented by the warm, attentive 5-star service. Our groups felt completely supported, deeply cherished, and truly cared for.

Following each retreat, Doug and I would spend a week exploring a different beach town, envisioning a potential future home in Costa Rica. During our last retreat, I suggested Montezuma, but Doug was keen on seeing Samara first. However, I had a strong intuition that Montezuma held something special for us.

My healing model continued to evolve and expand with each client I worked with, especially in online group settings. Each person's unique needs inspired me to create lessons and worksheets to help them. Childhood experiences, coping mechanisms, and the path to healing are deeply personal, shaped by individual awareness and previous therapeutic experiences.

I designed the process to be universally applicable, regardless of an individual's current healing stage or specific challenges. These challenges could include physical symptoms, depression, anxiety, eating disorders, addictions, codependency, and problematic relationship patterns and triggers.

Out of my own experiences of being overwhelmed and defeated by intense emotional triggers, I created the lessons I desperately needed, and these became a guide to healing that I now share.

I shared my teaching materials and methods with Doug, who confirmed that I had indeed developed a comprehensive healing model. His gift in organizing and modeling theoretical systems was invaluable. Doug's suggestion to call my emotional healing approach "Core Emotional Healing" was a light bulb moment, and it became the perfect name for the model. *Thank you, Doug.*

After two years of trying to conceive a child, we experienced our fifth miscarriage—my sixth—the same week I worked with my first group in my Core Emotional Healing online program. I realized the profound significance of this synchronicity: my heart had been broken wide open to hold the pain of others, and I embraced that this new program was my "baby," yearning to be born.

I channeled my energy into building my business, which shifted my focus away from wanting a baby. Any lingering desire for a child vanished one afternoon as we spent the day on our pool deck with Doug's grown children and his son's partner's young son.

While we occasionally babysat, a full day spent connecting with Doug's daughter and son, coupled with the realization that babysitting would cut into my much-needed downtime, solidified my decision: *I did not want a baby.*

This clarity brought me an enormous sense of relief, freedom, and peace. For the first time, I was absolutely certain that having a baby wasn't my path, and I knew I didn't have to think about it again.

When I told Doug, he gave me an amused look with his big, wide-open blue eyes and said, "That's what I was trying to tell you!" We both laughed and took a big sigh of relief.

I realized I already had two amazing "bonus" children through Doug—and they were exactly the kids I'd want. I felt incredibly blessed and content with my family and my business. I was already parenting Doug's children and all my clients. *I embraced my role as a nurturing heart mother to all.*

Sharing my work, insights, and processes with Doug was exhilarating. For the first time, I felt truly understood, seen, and reflected by another person. The hunger for validating and acknowledging my insights, experiences, and gifts was profound; it fueled another inner awakening. In a sense, my codependency with Doug served as a bridge to self-security. He became my mirror, reflecting what I offered to others and revealing the triggers I needed to heal myself.

GIRL GIRL

The first time I saw Girl, she was hiding in a hole she had dug under a concrete slab in a fenced outdoor cage. Her brindle fur was matted, and her big black eyes were filled with fear. She was fierce, yet fragile, hiding from the world that had failed her.

Just after Trump's first election, our indoor-outdoor cat, Toni, disappeared. While searching for our missing cat, Doug met a man who lived on the other side of the urban forest where we often walked our dogs.

The man showed Doug around his property and introduced him to his dog, Girl, who was confined to an outdoor cage. The hole she had dug under the concrete slab provided some sense of safety and shelter from Atlanta's harsh weather extremes.

Her owner joked that she was an architect, but Doug returned home heartbroken, both by the continued loss of Toni and Girl's living conditions. Girl and our dog Brocco shared a striking resemblance—both brindle-striped, with wise eyes and a certain jungle-like energy—so Doug was eager for me to meet her.

The next day, we walked Brocco over, and Girl perked up. She fell in love with Brocco at first sight. Initially timid with us, Girl quickly warmed up as we opened her gate and gave her love.

We visited Girl every day on our walk. If she saw Brocco first, she would come right up to her gate, but if she saw us in the distance, she would hide in her hole, afraid of humans. Each night, I'd fall asleep worrying about Girl, alone and cold on the hard ground, and tears would fill my eyes.

One week, I noticed she had no food left and looked starved, so I brought her food and fresh water. Concerned, I asked Doug to call her owner, who was nowhere to be seen. It turned out he had moved out to sell the house and was only dumping food in her small igloo twice a week.

When Doug spoke to him, he'd been in the hospital for two weeks and hadn't told anyone to feed Girl. She was eleven years old with many health problems, and I think he was expecting her to die.

Doug asked if he wanted us to find Girl a new home, and he agreed. That day, Mother's Day, I took videos and photos of Girl and posted them on my Facebook wall and in neighborhood groups, hoping to find her a foster home. Taking her in ourselves felt overwhelming; Molly was already seventeen, blind, deaf, and needed a lot of care. Plus, Brocco wasn't happy when we adopted Molly when she was fourteen. It all felt like too much, but I did my best to find Girl a good home.

The next day at home, Girl's abandonment by her owner triggered my deep-seated childhood wounds. I cried and cried, realizing it was similar to what I experienced with my father. There were no specific memories, just a deep well of grief that I'd never accessed.

Though not physically abandoned, I'd been emotionally abandoned and mistreated, and in that moment, I didn't need to analyze it; I just needed to feel. The intensity of the emotional response was overwhelming, and I found myself uncontrollably grieving for two days straight.

Doug didn't know how to support me through this. I don't think anyone could have helped me; I just needed to allow myself to feel it fully. The first day, I spent the entire day in our sunroom, crying and wailing.

The next day, still raw and emotionally fragile, I went to Pilates. When a woman asked about my progress in finding a home for Girl, it triggered another wave of grief. I left Pilates and sat in my car in the Trader Joe's parking lot, sobbing uncontrollably and unable to go inside.

Your triggers are a gift; they are healing opportunities echoed in my mind from my trigger lesson. They come from other people, and even our pets, to help us heal when we are ready.

Lying awake at night, I knew *I had to get her.* The next day, Doug brought gourmet raw meat to lure her into my car, but after taking a bite, she bolted back to her pen. Girl sensed that we wanted to take her away and became fearful. Her pen was all she knew. She felt safe in her isolation, despite the misery.

We chased her around the outside of her pen for an hour. Finally, Doug was able to catch her. He held her gently between his legs while we calmed her with water and wiped away her tears. Then, he put Girl in my car, I got in, and we looked deeply into each other's souls.

I thought about how scared she was to leave the only place she knew, even though it wasn't good for her. She was scared of the unknown, and I was also unsure how she would be when I brought her home from the vet.

Girl was so good at the vet, her first check-up and first time outside of her cage. Driving home, I felt proud of my brave Girl Girl, as I loved to call her. I carried her from the car into our fenced yard, where she initially hid under the deck.

Eventually, she emerged, and Doug guided her into the house. I gave her her first shower and brushed her wild fur until she indicated she'd had enough by letting out a small growl, showing me her teeth.

I noticed she had clear boundaries, and I respected that about her. It had been a big, stressful day for her, so she settled into "The Spa" on the rug and didn't want to leave.

That night, I guided her outside to go potty. She quickly relieved herself and ran back to her sanctuary in the bathroom, furthest from any outside doors. The next evening, she found comfort on a towel in our sunroom. It took some encouragement to get her outside again, and even then, she came right back in after a quick pee.

After a few days, she ventured into the backyard with Doug and Brocco for longer periods. The truth was, Girl had always longed to be inside, surrounded by people and dogs. As she settled in, she became calm, and the wild, fearful look in her eyes gradually disappeared.

She was scared, but her fear stemmed from abandonment and betrayal, not from us, her rescuers. She initially projected her fear onto us because she felt unsafe.

I reflected on how many people avoid emotional work out of fear rooted in the past, even when there's little to fear in the present. This past fear creates defenses that distort the truth, like "I'm happy as I am" or "I've already dealt with that."

For a long time, I believed my emotional "cage" was safe, retreating into it when things got tough. It provided a false sense of protection but also prevented me from what I truly needed and desired. Facing my fear and allowing myself to feel my emotions ultimately brought me safety, security, and the love I had always craved.

I saw myself more clearly through Girl. Rescuing her was like rescuing my inner child. I realized what a powerful example, healer, and source of love she was for me. She showed me that it's never too late to get the love you want, and I deserved the best. Girl claimed a cozy bed in every room, her big, dark eyes pouring love into me as we healed each other with our strong, warrior hearts.

Girl had a large throat tumor, a dozen dead teeth, enlarged ovaries, and advanced heartworm. After the initial surgery, she underwent six months of heartworm treatment followed by a year of high-quality supplements and food to aid her organ recovery.

When Girl was ready for walks, I was initially worried about how she'd do on a leash, but I quickly realized she didn't need any training; she was simply happy to be by my side.

One day, Doug walked the dogs without me and encountered Girl's former owner. Surprised to see she was alive, he was hurt that she didn't greet him excitedly. He explained that she usually ran to him and he would knock her on the head with his knuckles. Girl ignored him and continued walking, demonstrating her clear boundaries with the man who had mistreated her.

Girl had lost her voice before we met, her barks unanswered. Hearing her find it again brought me immense joy, barking alongside Brocco and greeting me each morning with the cutest seal sound.

Her eyes spoke volumes of love and appreciation, and we shared a deep understanding. I knew what she needed and provided it; she did the same for me. My Girl Girl is always with me in my heart.

With Girl by my side, I was building my business, which was exhilarating. I poured my energy into producing YouTube videos, writing blogs, speaking on podcasts, contributing to two collaborative bestsellers, and working with unwavering dedication. Even during my downtime, my conversations with Doug revolved around the model and process, which constantly evolved.

My first Facebook Live video, filmed on a beautiful sunny winter day in Atlanta, was on using emotional triggers for healing—a key lesson in the Core Emotional

Healing process. Setting up my phone on our leaf-covered pool deck, I felt a nervous flutter: there would be no stopping or editing if I stumbled.

Despite my nerves, I passionately shared how recognizing and utilizing triggers is an invaluable healing skill, reviewing the types I teach—unhealed childhood wounds, shadow projections, and boundary violations—and concluding with an invitation to my first in-person workshop on triggers.

Many people commented on the video to thank me, praising the wisdom, authenticity, and usefulness of the information. One woman even remarked on the genuine love I radiated for people.

Doug, always an enthusiastic supporter of my work, was eager to see me in action, so I invited him to my workshop. In a rented local yoga studio, we arranged folding chairs in a circle for the dozen attendees. Doug assisted by distributing my handouts as I began teaching about the various triggers and how to recognize them.

When I opened up the sharing portion, a woman immediately delved into the intense emotional triggers from her relationship with her husband, stemming back to childhood. The friend she brought to the workshop sat beside her, and her triggers clearly resonated with his relationship triggers.

Without a word, Doug and I fell into a seamless rhythm, guiding the pair to engage in dialogue—each mirroring the other's partner or parent. The power of the experience was undeniable, and we continued to work with each participant in this intuitive, collaborative way.

Afterward, I turned to Doug, beaming joyfully, "That was fun, let's do more of that."

Equally excited and surprised, he replied, "I can't believe we never discussed our shared expertise and passion for experiential therapy."

Doug's background in Gestalt and experiential therapy, including leading an experiential retreat during his PhD, and my extensive experience assisting in experiential courses and developing my methods during retreats, had naturally converged in that transformative workshop.

Since triggers were an ongoing theme in our relationship, we followed up the workshop with a Facebook Live video titled "Conscious Relating: Transforming Conflict and Distance into Love," where we shared personal examples of healing through our triggers.

The video instantly had thousands of views and eighty comments requesting our help and more content, ultimately leading us to host our radio show, "The Intimacy Hour." Additionally, Doug contributed articles on conscious relating to the Good Men Project and established a supportive men's group on Facebook.

GYPSY CARNIVAL

For my forty-fourth birthday, Doug gave me one of the best gifts imaginable. He rented my dream home overlooking the ocean in Santa Teresa, Costa Rica.

When he first suggested I look at the Airbnb listing while we were in Atlanta, I initially refused, saying, "We can't afford it," when he told me the price.

But he persisted, asking again and again. *I do love his persistence.* When I finally looked at the listing, I immediately said YES. It was the most incredible house I had ever seen. Once we both decided to rent it, things started falling into place; clients and business came to us, supporting our decision.

This was the first year in three years that I wasn't offering our retreat. Instead, Doug and I were offering private experiential healing immersions. My client, Anna, who lived in Montezuma (thirty minutes away from Santa Teresa), booked a private healing immersion after completing my online programs. Since we would be in Santa Teresa for my birthday, I told Anna we would come to her for the immersion.

We spent a week in Montezuma before heading to my dream home. The immersion with Anna was profound, not only for her personal growth but also for our future collaboration. Working with plants and flowers, Anna distills their essences into formulas specifically designed for emotional healing.

Upon her arrival at our Airbnb, we hugged, and she applied her release formula to prepare for the immersion. I felt its power instantly. Watching Anna work with her formulas reflected how I developed my process—as she handed me the Sacred Lotus, I realized how love and transformation come in many forms, and I was being opened to a new way of healing.

Anna and I saw how her formulas perfectly complemented the Core Emotional Healing (CEH) process, and she created a CEH kit for my clients to use. The formulas help drop defenses, reconnect with repressed memories and emotions, and rediscover our true selves.

After Anna's immersion, Doug and I explored Montezuma as a potential place to live. The small bohemian beach town was alive with energy. Tattooed artisans with dreadlocks sold their macramé jewelry and musicians played wooden African drums, while fire performers entertained the crowds. The atmosphere was reminiscent of a gypsy carnival, with free spirits filling the streets. On our way to the beach, we stopped at a restaurant for refreshing papaya, pineapple, and ginger smoothies.

We discovered a mile-long sand beach called Playa Grande that was best for swimming at the end of a thirty-minute walk through a nature preserve. As we walked, the natural beauty of the jungle, ocean, and rocks captivated me. My body and soul sang with delight, and I exclaimed to Doug, "I love this. I love this walk, I love it so much!"

We stopped halfway at Piedra Colorada, a cove where a small waterfall in a river forms a freshwater pool. "Piedra" means "stone" in Spanish, and "Colorada" translates to "colorful"—the riverbed is lined with vibrantly colored jasper stones. Visitors and locals stack different-sized stones to create beautiful collaborative natural sculptures.

A small brindle-coated dog approached me as I spread my sarong on the sand. He looked exactly like a miniature version of our dogs, Brocco and Girl, combined. I went to the ocean to tell Doug. When I looked back, the little dog was comfortably nestled on my sarong. I knew this was a sign.

I was so excited to be in my dream home in Santa Teresa that we ended up leaving Montezuma a day early. The drive was bumpy, along winding dirt roads filled with dust and ditches. As we drove into Santa Teresa, it looked the same as I remembered from our first retreat, but much busier with more houses, people, cars, motorbikes, and ATVs carrying surfboards.

After driving up a steep hill from the beach, we arrived at the house, and my jaw dropped. Its unique and stunning modern architecture and design completely overwhelmed me. The second floor had an open kitchen and living room with panoramic ocean views that extended even to the hallway's open wall.

Walking down the length of the house to the light and spacious master bedroom, I saw a mermaid painting on the wall and felt an immediate connection. Stepping onto the large deck off the master bedroom, I took in the expansive ocean view and never wanted to leave. I turned to Doug and said, "Let's manifest this house."

A Quan Yin statue greeted me at the bottom of the stairs, which opened onto the pool deck and second bedroom. It took me two full days to truly receive this luxurious space. This house wasn't merely a space; it was a symbol of abundance and beauty that I had, for years, doubted I deserved. But, at that moment, I felt ready to receive it all.

The magical energy and clarity of the Nicoya Peninsula quickly revealed the ongoing issues and tension between us. Doug's driving often made me feel unsafe, and I would repeatedly ask him to slow down, which he would do for a short while, and eventually, I would usually drive.

He would also sometimes defend himself by pointing out he'd never been in an accident, and when I reiterated "I don't feel safe," he would acknowledge this, but I felt he did so in a way that dismissed my concerns and made it my issue.

After coffee and breakfast, we drove to the farmers' market across from the beach. Doug was driving too fast, and someone had to wave him down and yell for him to slow down. I turned to him and said, "See, it's not just me."

Shortly after, he pulled into a dirt area before the farmers market, despite clear signs prohibiting cars. I warned him not to enter, but he ignored me. Ultimately, someone had to tell him to leave, and I felt unheard.

This brought me back into my childhood wounds, where my feelings and my truth never mattered. I let it go, but it sat heavy in my chest. I felt a similar sting of being dismissed deep in my stomach from my needs and feelings being silenced as a child. This was a pattern I was trying to break, but it felt like an uphill battle within from my conditioning to just *let it go*.

Back at my dream house, I jumped into the plunge pool to wash off the tension. As the sun dipped below the horizon, casting vibrant orange and red hues across the ocean, we found a moment of peace watching the breathtaking sunset.

On previous Costa Rica vacations, the beach had been the most relaxing part of our trip. This time, simply enjoying the house on the hill, pool, and view brought us peace. Feeling calm, relaxed, and inspired, I turned to Doug and said, "Let's move here. Let's make it happen now."

Doug agreed, "Yes, let's do it. We always feel better in Costa Rica than Atlanta."

I messaged my new friend Anna in Montezuma and asked her, "How do we find long-term places to rent in this area?"

She replied, "Amazing timing, my next-door neighbors just asked me if I knew anyone who would want to rent their newly constructed house with a pool for six months next year, starting in February." That synchronicity was confirmation for us to do it.

The timing couldn't have been more perfect for us to go home, find a renter for our house, clear it out, sell our cars, and make all the arrangements to move with our dogs in a few months.

DISNEY MOVIE

After all the planning and purging, we finally boarded the plane to create our new life in Costa Rica. "We did it!" I said to Doug, and we both exclaimed while laughing, "Pura Fu**ing Vida," as we waved goodbye to Atlanta.

Arriving in Montezuma with our two dogs, Brocco and Girl, and our lives packed into overstuffed suitcases, I was captivated by the relaxing and nourishing jungle energy. There was an instantaneous knowing we were there to stay, no need for a trial.

Doug turned to me and said, "Let's go find our home." Having completed a manifestation program two years prior, we already had a clear vision for our dream house: a hilltop sanctuary with panoramic ocean views and an infinity pool.

I asked our landlord for realtor recommendations, and he connected us with Rachel. After sending her a description of our dream home, she sent me a listing that seemed to fit what we wanted. However, viewing the property was challenging due to numerous obstacles put in place by the renters, who were from the US.

After a month and a dozen disappointing viewings, I contacted Rachel again. I urged her to inform the owner that the current tenants were hindering viewings and potentially jeopardizing the sale. This intervention secured us a viewing.

Rachel drove us up the winding, grassy driveway, where palm trees and red hibiscus lined one side with breathtaking ocean views, and pink bougainvillea lined the other side that went up the hill to the house. As we stepped out of the car, the infinity pool going straight out to the panoramic deep blue ocean took our breath away.

Though the renters initially obstructed the full view from the house and porch, the property's energy stayed with us. A second viewing, without the renters present, revealed even more of the home and land's unique features.

Walking around the property, I saw the expansive vistas of the sparkling Pacific Ocean, the lush Costa Rican mainland, and its majestic mountain ranges. The beauty overwhelmed me. I turned to Doug and mouthed *Oh my God*, and he nodded in awe.

Looking out to the ocean from the front porch, I gazed down the hill to the large front area of the property filled with mature fruit trees. There were citrus, starfruit, banana, coconut, and a large jackfruit tree.

As I took a deep breath, I smelled the relaxing aromatherapy of the ylang-ylang framing the side of the house. I sat down to take it all in, and a vibrant green and blue hummingbird hovered in front of me, confirming *this is our home*.

Behind the house was a small garden with orchids along the trunk of an almond tree and a path down the hillside that descended into the wild jungle with more fruit trees—avocado, mango, and two different kinds of limes. It was truly a tropical oasis.

With the house opened up, each of the three rooms showcased the ocean view through the large sliding glass doors. I turned to Doug, "We can watch the sunrise and moonrise over the ocean from our bed. This is even better than my dream house in Santa Teresa." I knew in my bones that it wasn't just a dream home, it was home.

The property was quiet, peaceful, and private but not isolated. Above the beach, it was located between and away from the main towns. The first time we went to that beach, I felt a special energy before I knew houses existed on this hill.

I asked a woman on the beach where she lived, and she pointed up to where this house is. Later, I discovered that she lives on the same street, becoming our neighbor and solidifying my connection to this place.

Manifesting our dream house wasn't easy. The six months following the contract signing tested our trust and patience as we navigated Costa Rican laws, processes, and the inevitable initiation into expat life.

Despite the hurdles, I held onto the intuitive feeling that everything would unfold in perfect timing. We were fortunate to have a wonderful place to stay during the wait.

Montezuma was fun. Every time we left our house, we would meet interesting people, rebels, innovators, mystics, and artists—perhaps the most self-actualized people in one small bohemian town.

Each Friday morning, we packed up for a Playa Grande day, which involved stuffing Doug's CamelBak backpack with water, snacks, sarongs, Brocco's leash, and a frisbee.

My favorite coastal walk began at Montezuma Beach, past Ylang Ylang Beach Resort, and along the nature reserve's trails. With cliffs going out to the ocean and large crashing waves on the rocks, the path led us through diverse beaches with unique landscapes, before finally reaching Playa Grande.

Playa Grande's energy was special; the untouched jungle and the vast ocean cleansed and healed me, whispering messages in the rhythm of the waves.

As I lay on the sand, soothed by the surf, I reflected on my last healing session with Rebecca: "Seize the moment and you will be in alignment in Costa Rica. Your tribe is there; you will meet your twin soul and have many talks on the beach, more and more people will be coming, angels in human form to guide you further, and a little girl who you will meet with brown eyes will look up at you and she will say, "You are my mom now."

I didn't know what she meant by that, but I kept open.

On our walk back from our "church," as a soulful man in the community fondly called Playa Grande, we'd stop at Ylang Ylang for a sunset dinner. Sipping our spirulina pineapple ginger smoothies by the beach, I playfully nudged Doug. "Remember those dog walks in Atlanta, grabbing burritos at Elmyriachi with a barbershop view?"

We chuckled, still amazed that we now called this tropical paradise home.

The feeling continued as we drove through our quirky new town on the beach. Laughing with joy, "This is our neighborhood!" Back at our temporary haven, we would jump into the pool and wash away the salty ocean, the perfect end to our Playa Grande day.

A neighbor mentioned a Sound Journey offered by Patricia at Ylang Ylang every Thursday afternoon. Her healing sessions incorporated Alchemy Crystal bowls, Sun and Venus Gongs, a Hapi Drum, Crystal Lyra, Koshi Chimes, and a variety of other instruments, including her voice and the soothing sounds of the sea.

The Sound Journey became our Thursday ritual, transporting us to another realm with our soul tribe. Playa Grande, the community, and the magic of this place resonated deeply with my soul—I felt like I had finally come home.

I needed a haircut, so I contacted Jane, the best hairdresser in Montezuma. As we pulled into Jane's driveway, her five dogs greeted us with an off-key chorus of barks, joined by three more from Char's tiny home nestled at the top of the property. One of Char's dogs, River, immediately gravitated toward me, forming an instant bond.

We soon discovered that Jane and her husband Lee were practically neighbors, living just two houses down from our potential dream home. The connection deepened when we learned that the original owners of both houses are sisters, and they created a path that led directly to the enchanted garden in the back of our desired house.

Through Jane, our hairdresser and newfound friend, we quickly immersed ourselves in an active social scene, a first for us as a couple. Our introverted Atlanta days were gone as we attended house parties and live music nights in Montezuma and Cabuya three to four times per week.

The community, a melting pot of artists and mystic misfits, offered a constant stream of open mics and bands, igniting our creative sparks. Doug's harmonica skills landed him a spot playing with the local legend, Congo, and I even found the courage to join them on stage one night, playing the djembe drum.

On the weekends, there was an organic market during the day and fire shows and drumming at night. I loved dancing in the street with our tribe. I felt truly alive, and for the first time, perhaps, a sense of belonging.

Doug had been a professional improv comedian in Atlanta, and I had just completed level two improv training before our move to Costa Rica. Our shared quick wit and natural synergy, honed through our experiential therapy immersions, translated seamlessly to the stage.

With our creative energy ignited, Doug reached out to the Montezuma community via Facebook, seeking fellow improv enthusiasts. In no time, we formed the first improv troupe in the area, practiced diligently twice a week, and within two months, we were performing weekly shows. Our social life went from zero to 100 within the first six months of living in Montezuma.

As I had intuitively felt, the timing of our house closing aligned perfectly. We attended Doug's son's wedding in Atlanta, and upon our return, we closed on our dream home. This allowed us to efficiently handle both the wedding and the complete clearing out of our Atlanta house in a single trip, preparing it for sale. Our Atlanta chapter closed seamlessly as our dream life in Costa Rica unfolded.

Living in our dream home surpassed our wildest dreams. At five in the morning, the howler monkeys' calls would rhythmically wake us from sleep. We'd settle into our gravity chairs on the pool deck with coffee in hand, watching the sunrise paint the sky with vibrant hues. Afterward, I would take a dip in our pool that Doug converted to salt, doing my signature handstand walk and upside-down Pilates morning ritual.

During the day, hundreds of dragonflies flitted around the pool deck. Toucans feasted on papaya in our trees, and hummingbirds and butterflies danced in the tropical flowers. Rain showers would leave double rainbows curving across the sky, framing our expansive view.

Each evening, we relaxed in our gravity chairs, witnessing the sunset's reflection shimmer across the water from Santa Teresa, the moon rising, and the sky covered with stars. Doug would count how many shooting stars he saw, and I would say, "We live in a Disney movie."

The infinity pool and expansive ocean view continued to amaze us each time we emerged from the back of the house or stepped out of our car. Our dream home was truly a sanctuary.

Returning from town always brought an instant wave of relaxation and contentment. Thanks to the original owner's design, the house's elevation and natural breeze kept it cool and comfortable, free from excessive heat and insects.

I felt a sense of liberation as I gazed out at the ocean, watching as the vultures, caracaras, parrots, macaws, falcons, hawks, motmots, toucans, and hummingbirds soared past at eye level throughout the day.

Mesmerized by the vultures soaring, I danced on the patio, grabbed my medicine drum, and a song flowed out.

> The wind blows on the land,
> vultures gliding,
> because they can.
> Waves of emotion,
> flowing through my body.
>
> We feel it all,
> we feel it all,
> we feel it all,
> right
> here.

Your true nature
is calling you.
Are you listening,
to your feelings too?

We feel it all,
we feel it all,
we feel it all,
right
here.

Char's dog, River, claimed our patio as her own the moment we moved in. While I felt a strong connection, as if she were destined to be mine, River left no doubt that she had chosen me as her new Mama.

One day, while adding photos of River to my dog album, I suddenly remembered Rebecca's prediction about a little girl with brown eyes who would declare, "You are my mom now." My heart smiled, realizing that she meant River. *Of course, she's a dog.* River and I express the same big love and joy and have a lot of fun playing and cuddling together.

While Char adored River and wished for her to stay, she graciously acknowledged, "She makes her own decisions." Girl and Brocco welcomed River into our pack with open paws. River, a truly lovable dog, found herself surrounded by love from all sides. With her puppy-like joy and exuberance, I affectionately nicknamed her Baby Puppy.

Not only did we manifest our dream home, but I also manifested Baby Puppy. She reminded me of my college days, when I had a cherished stuffed dog named Puppy Face, and my then-boyfriend had one we called Doggie Face.

A lifetime later, in Atlanta, where none of our dogs were cuddlers, I confessed to Doug in bed, "I long for an eternal puppy who loves to cuddle."

WISDOM'S TEARS

Just as we closed on our house, we received an invitation to audition for a new reality TV show called *Welcome to the Jungle*. The show focused on married couples in the US who decided to leave their old lives behind and move to the jungles of Central America.

The director selected us for the first episode because she was intrigued by our healing work, our motivations for moving to Costa Rica, and our life in Montezuma. Our episode was titled "Finding Healing in Costa Rica."

Filming was a lot of fun, along with very long hours, for four days straight. We showcased our house. They used a drone to video us in the pool with our view of the ocean, and the adventurous drives we took on dirt roads through rivers.

We included highlights of our new life, such as the sound healing and lunch at Ylang Ylang on the beach, the fire and drum performances in town, and our favorite full moon beach bonfire with friends and music.

A few weeks after we finished filming, the COVID outbreak shut down the world. Borders closed, the show's production was canceled, and the crew returned to the US. While disappointing, this was the least of our concerns.

Doug's forensic evaluation cases in Atlanta, which required him to fly back every three months, were postponed.

Since everyone was stuck at home without distractions, many who had been putting off healing now had the time and space to confront their inner discomfort. As my clients increased significantly, I asked Doug to join me in assisting.

I created and taught an online class that included my Core Emotional Healing Self Study course, which covered one step of the Core Emotional Healing process each week and became a prerequisite for the longer program. The class had a waitlist, and I even set up a training program for practitioners to support future growth.

Bringing Doug into my business worked well, as he helped develop the Core Emotional Healing model and, in practice, added a great deal with his clinical experience, intuition, and training as a psychologist.

As we worked together, we learned from each other and complemented each other's skills and expertise.

Montezuma shut down, and the beaches were closed off. The timing of our move couldn't have been more perfect for us to be "stuck" at our dream home.

Our days fell into a simple rhythm: coffee at sunrise, my pool ritual, supporting groups on Zoom and online forums, dog walks, and spending late afternoons in conversation.

Some local chefs even delivered food to our house—delicious sourdough, gourmet fresh sushi, bean soups, and kombucha. Our home transformed into a private 5-star wellness retreat. We were aware of the stark contrast between our situation and that of others, particularly the locals who suddenly found themselves without work or food. We did our best to help those in need.

Suddenly, our lively nightlife vanished, and we were back to just the two of us. The solitude of 2020 brought clarity for many, myself included. I realized which friendships no longer resonated, and as a sensitive introvert, I didn't miss the constant social interaction. In reflection, our previously busy social life had been a distraction from our ongoing relationship issues.

Girl passed away. Doug buried her down our back hill in the jungle, near the stream, planting purple flowers on her grave.

I grieved her deeply. Not having her presence and big, seal-like eyes pouring unconditional love into me every day left a significant void.

We had extended her life by four years, giving her a loving home with everything she ever wanted and needed. She experienced a loving family who cared for her, the beauty of a tropical jungle life outdoors, the comfort of cuddling back-to-back with her buddy Brocco, fresh meat treats, and a comfy bed indoors. Eventually, I had a stuffed dog made to look just like her, which helped me maintain a connection to my Girl Girl.

When the world reopened, I chose to stay in while Doug ventured out to enjoy the town's nightlife. This newfound independence allowed us to address our codependency.

I focused on my creative expression through photography, capturing the beautiful birds in flight while sitting on our porch. I particularly loved photographing hummingbirds with their vibrant colors and swift wing movements. When I shared my photos on social media, the community adored these images of the tiny, iridescent jewels.

When a friend from Atlanta visited Montezuma with her boyfriend, she asked about horse therapy in the area. Although I hadn't experienced it, it piqued my interest, so I sent her the Horse Spirit Healing website.

After spending a day at the Resonance Ranch, she called me raving about it. "Elicia, you have to try it. Leticia works just like the leader from the course, but with horses."

I didn't have a specific issue in mind, but out of curiosity, I booked a private Equine Gestalt Session, open to whatever the horses might reveal.

The Resonance Ranch was conveniently located just ten minutes down the hill from our house. Upon arrival, I was greeted by Leticia's warm smile and captivated by her crystal-clear blue eyes.

We sat for tea at her house on the ranch, where she shared the history of the horses and their innate heart-healing power. She explained the Gestalt process and how to remain present with the horses as they intuitively moved around me, reflecting what I needed to see within myself.

As we approached the gate, the meditating horses shifted and repositioned themselves. Suddenly, Chocolate bolted out of the back gate, prompting Leticia to remark, "Oh, you must have good boundaries. Chocolate isn't needed here."

Joy, another horse, turned and locked eyes with me. Leticia opened the gate, inviting me to enter slowly. Initially, I felt awkward and uncertain, but Leticia skillfully reflected what she sensed the horses and I were communicating—a hesitancy stemming from a lack of self-trust and a fear of making mistakes.

Leticia's questions gently guided me to open up about my relationship and our recent conflicts. The herd leader, a majestic brown horse named Wisdom, approached and nudged his head on the top of mine. Leticia interpreted this as Wisdom guiding me to ground myself and connect with my body.

As I sat on the dirt, feeling a shift within, Wisdom cried tears into my hand and drew me close to his throat. Leticia explained that my throat and heart were closed, that I carried sadness from being made to feel wrong, which made me doubt myself even when I felt clear.

Both Wisdom and Joy reacted by gesturing as if to bite my left leg, mirroring the pain these patterns caused me. I felt exhausted and defeated by the weight of this recurring cycle.

As the sun set, we wrapped up the five-hour session. I left feeling deeply affected and went straight to sleep when I got home. I woke up at three in the morning with the emotions and insights from the session flooding my awareness.

I went to another room and cried for a long time. I vowed to address any issues that arose immediately rather than suppress or dismiss them. I was no longer willing to give up or let things slide. I realized that I desired, above all, to feel safe being myself.

That Christmas, both adult kids came to celebrate with us. It was the best time we had had as a family, a direct result of the individual and collective healing we had accomplished over the past eight years. They both expressed gratitude for my role in healing their family dynamics and for always supporting them and their path.

For the first time, we all felt safe enough to speak up when something bothered us. This newfound openness allowed our time together to be free and fun. We even took creative family photos on the edge of our infinity pool, capturing our individual personalities and the reflections of our joy and freedom in the water. That experience, along with a delicious lunch at our favorite restaurant, Playa de los Artistas, was the best Christmas gift imaginable.

TOXIC HOPE

Despite not spending all my time with Doug socially anymore, I still lacked close local friends. I especially craved girl time, so when a woman I knew from the community, Phoebe, invited me to Holly's birthday brunch, I was overjoyed.

Excitement coursed through me. *This is exactly what I need.* I knew and liked the other women Holly invited, and the brunch was intimate and during the day, which was ideal for me.

We were each asked to bring a brunch dish, prosecco, or juice. I made a kale quinoa salad and brought rosé—and a gift for Holly: a Reiki-charged protection spray with sage.

That first gathering of the six of us sparked a deep, fun, and uplifting connection. We shared similar personalities, interests, and expressions—talking openly and honestly, without judgment or reservation.

The food we brought complemented each other beautifully, creating a truly stunning brunch. I captured the spread and candid moments with photos, including a fabulous group shot. Afterward, we danced around the house and in the pool to a Spotify playlist.

I knew all the women at the brunch except Caitlin. She sat directly across from me at the table, and as we ate and talked, I was struck by what she was saying to another woman. It was exactly what I would say. She offered support directly, clearly, and with empowering encouragement.

I had never met someone so similar to me, and it was refreshing to relax and not have to fill that role for once. She was also incredibly funny, quick-witted, tall, and we even looked similar. After brunch, she created a WhatsApp group, branding us the "Magical Friends." We all wanted to get together again soon—our time together had nourished us all.

My birthday was approaching in less than a month, so we decided to have another brunch then. In the meantime, we stayed connected through our WhatsApp group and added to our Spotify playlist. As the only Apple Music user, I struggled with it, jokingly calling it "Spotif*cked." Caitlin cracked up, noting our shared sense of humor.

I felt alive with our connection, and Doug was happy that I'd finally found friends I truly connected with, shared interests with, and who provided a social outlet separate from our relationship.

Beyond monthly brunches, we danced together in Santa Teresa and watched our friend Caroline spin fire at Rancho Itauna. One night in Montezuma, Caitlin joined Doug and me dancing. As she and I moved together near the DJ while Doug socialized elsewhere, I noticed our synchronicity and the energy I felt around her. It highlighted the contrast in my energy levels when I was with Doug.

Our frequent efforts to change our difficult dynamic left me drained. The cause of my fatigue was often unclear. This experience with Caitlin showed me that the problem wasn't what I was or wasn't doing; despite little sleep, I felt energized the next day.

Caitlin and I quickly formed a deep bond, messaging each other day and night. We both craved connection and validation of our feelings and experiences.

One day on the beach, we discussed the possibility of a twin soul connection, and I shared Rebecca's prediction from years prior—before I even moved to Costa Rica—that I would meet my twin and have long talks with her on the beach.

Before our connection, I often found myself alone on the couch at night while Doug slept, writing and processing my feelings in my Notes app. Finally, I had someone who truly understood me, who mirrored my truth back to me. We even found joy in creating silly parody songs together. This shift changed everything for me and Doug, who wasn't happy about it.

I spoke up more and processed our issues all the time while spending less time with Doug. The focus was on him and my desire for change, and I wasn't sharing everything with only him anymore.

This combination and more combusted into a major blowout fight the night before Caitlin and I were leaving for a weekend trip to San Jose for a dentist appointment and house supplies.

In the heat of that late-night argument, we both uttered truths about not being compatible. The realization that this signaled the end left me utterly paralyzed by fear.

The next day, during our drive, I was in a state of shock from the fight and the realization that our marriage was ending. I knew we weren't compatible anymore, and I needed Caitlin's reflection and validation of my feelings.

At our Airbnb, while recounting the challenges in our relationship, I turned to Caitlin and said, "I think I had toxic hope." Tilting my head, I asked, "Is that even a thing?"

A quick Google search led me to a *Psychology Today* article—it was indeed a thing. Things had been difficult, yet I held tightly to the hope that they could change, even when they never did. I would focus on what I perceived as change, but it wasn't real. This realization and the decision it led to were gut-wrenching.

I returned home and asked for a separation, suggesting we read *Conscious Uncoupling*. I lay in bed and cried nonstop for a week. I couldn't believe our marriage and shared dreams were ending. Even though we were already sleeping in separate rooms, I yearned for a solitude that could bring clarity. I needed more time and space alone to heal and ensure this was the right decision.

The Caribbean coast of Costa Rica had been calling me for years, and now was the time to answer, alone. I had to stay in Montezuma for a couple more weeks to complete scheduled essence photo shoots, so I dog sat at two friends' houses to give myself the space I needed.

One night, at the first house, something nudged me awake at midnight. Startled, I checked my phone and found a flurry of messages from Doug—Brocco was missing. I messaged him back immediately, promising to help search in the morning. I fell back asleep and dreamt of Brocco walking along an enchanted path, asking directions from horses before continuing. Upon waking, I had a feeling the dream meant he had crossed over, but I pushed the thought aside until I tried to find him.

At sunrise, I went to our house and searched for Brocco, first by car, then on foot. Doug and I were devastated, and we suspected he went into the jungle to die peacefully before his health deteriorated further. At fourteen, he was struggling with his sight and mobility. I couldn't help but feel he also chose this path to ease my departure, as we were deeply bonded as each other's nurturers.

I took the opportunity at our house to tell Doug that I was going to the Caribbean coast for a month to heal and gain clarity. "I feel like I need to fly," I explained, expressing my need to leave and explore new horizons independently.

At that moment, as I stepped from our kitchen onto the patio, twelve scarlet macaws soared from the coast directly toward me and overhead. They had become my favorite birds to photograph over the past year, and I knew this was a sign, affirming my decision.

Knowing Brocco's time was limited, we got another young male dog for Doug a year earlier. When he first slept with us, I woke up at three in the morning, turned to Doug, and asked, "Is Doggie Boy here?" He said yes, realizing that was my nickname for Rocket. I didn't make the connection to my college boyfriend and our two stuffed dogs, Puppy Face and Doggie Face, until much later.

River and Rocket quickly became inseparable, constantly playing and cuddling. The thought of leaving them for a month was difficult, and the idea of eventually separating them was unbearable.

My only focus was to be alone on the Caribbean coast. As Madonna's "Isaac" played in my head, its haunting melody and spiritual lyrics ignited a deep knowing within me. I needed to go somewhere new and heal.

SHAKING THE TREE

Riding in the taxi through Puerto Viejo on Costa Rica's Caribbean coast on my way to my Airbnb, I felt a shift. The jungle was different here—ancient trees, thick with vines, felt truly wild. The turquoise ocean was calm and sparkly, and the long, flat road connecting the towns felt like a welcoming path. Even with my inner stress, a deep peace settled over me. The Caribbean embraced me with a warm hug.

Rozi, with her vibrant turquoise hair and an aura of magical, loving energy, greeted me as I arrived at Villas Elementos in Playa Chiquita. Unsure which villa would be mine for the month, I followed her to my Airbnb, Villa Gaia—Mother Earth.

Stepping into the terra cotta building felt like entering the earth's womb. In Playa Chiquita, "little girl" entering Mother Earth's womb, I immediately knew my inner child was here for deep healing and nurturing.

The first night was unsettling. My trauma felt raw and exposed, and I was without my usual comforts—my dogs, my dream home, and familiar faces.

The jungle's symphony was overwhelming. Unlike my Montezuma home, where the absence of overhead trees ensured a quiet night, here, hard fruits and branches crashed onto the metal roof, jolting me awake with a surge of fear.

The howler monkey calls were louder, wilder, and more intense than the soothing rhythmic sounds on the other coast. I felt utterly immersed in the earth, the jungle, and the depths of my trauma.

That first morning, while we drank coffee, I told Rozi I was on a retreat to heal. Immediately, she embraced me as a nurturing, loving, and empowering mother figure. She saw me completely, gave me the space I craved, and anticipated all my needs.

Rozi, trained by a Michelin-starred chef in Italy, also nourished me with gourmet meals during my most challenging moments. She seemed to understand my needs intuitively.

After securing a bicycle rental, Rozi and I went to the supermarket. It suddenly dawned on me that this was the first time in a decade I was shopping solely for myself. I was so accustomed to buying groceries for "us," for what *we* always ate.

It was a strange, almost surreal experience—a rediscovery of self through food. *What do I want to eat?* It felt like my very first time grocery shopping. I carefully examined each item, listening to my body's signals and allowing my intuition to guide me, filling the cart with ingredients to create meals designed just for me.

At sunrise, I lounged in the hammock chair on my porch, coffee warming my hands, gazing at the enormous tree beside me, dreaming of spotting a sloth.

After breakfast, I packed my bag and walked across the street to the secret wooden door. Unlocking it with Rozi's key, I stepped onto a magical "portal" path alive with the calls of howler monkeys high in the canopy, the flutter of blue morpho butterflies among the foliage, and the majestic flight of great green macaws singing "RAAK" overhead.

Emerging from the path, my bare feet landed on the soft sand beach. I walked out to float in the crystal clear ocean—my daily sanctuary.

Most evenings were filled with tears as I grieved the separation and the uncertainty surrounding our love and the dream home we had created. My dogs, especially Baby Puppy, were constantly on my mind. Leaving her was difficult, but I needed to focus on my own needs.

One evening, a Facebook video shared by a friend caught my eye—a clip from Peter Gabriel's "Secret World Live" tour. Then came "Shaking the Tree," a song unfamiliar to me, which surprised me given that I had grown up listening to Peter Gabriel with my dad. It was as if the music spoke directly to my soul, each verse resonating with my current experience and emotions.

I immediately grabbed my earphones and played it on repeat. I danced around my bed for over an hour, lost in the music. The song's vibrations pulsed through me, dislodging something deep within, and suddenly, a profound truth surfaced. I saw the armor of strength I had worn, and the clear, undeniable light of my innocence.

Dinner at Rozi's by the pool was just the start of an extraordinary evening. After sharing the song, we let the music play on shuffle, and each tune synced up with our conversation.

Walking back to Villa Gaia, the beam of my phone's flashlight revealed a jaguarundi sitting on the back corner of my patio—a close encounter with a wild cat that left me momentarily speechless. I didn't feel threatened because they don't attack humans, but I did go inside pretty quickly and straight to bed.

The jaguarundi's energy lingered as I lay down. Then, women in the distance chanted a tribal song, eerily intertwined with the sounds of the jaguarundi killing prey right outside my wall.

After a moment of silence, the women played and sang the Fugees' "Killing Me Softly With His Song." The whole experience felt like a bizarre, dreamlike sequence from a David Lynch film.

A dolphin boat trip to celebrate Lula's birthday was the start of something special. Lula and I had initially connected through Facebook in my Atlanta days, and with her living in Costa Rica, we remained in contact.

I had mentioned a few times that I wanted to visit Puerto Viejo. It turned out she was friends with Rozi, so we went together to meet the other women gathering on the beach.

Walking toward them, I felt a pull toward Hai. It felt like an instant, soul-deep recognition. When she asked why I was visiting from Montezuma, I answered without hesitation, "I'm deciding if I'm leaving my husband." Our lives seemed to mirror each other, and we became instant friends.

To ensure I was making the right decision about ending my marriage, I embarked on a three-day solo immersion in Villa Gaia. It was an inward journey, revisiting my childhood, reconnecting with buried feelings, and committing to staying present with them.

Completely isolating myself within the villa, avoiding conversation and technology, Rozi provided me three meals a day, allowing me to fully immerse myself in my internal process.

I needed to confront the moments and reasons I had shut down my feelings, especially after experiencing abuse, to truly process and not just "forget about it" and "let it go."

With props, I unleashed my emotions, speaking fully and directly to each family member, using physical objects to represent them and enhance my expression. The next day, I danced for hours to empowering music. During this three-hour movement, it became clear that I wasn't ready to return to Montezuma.

As I danced, the thought arose: *I should go back soon; my dogs need me.*

But then, I countered to myself, *They're fine. They're together with their dad and happy at home with room to roam.*

I paused, then affirmed, *No, I'm not going back yet. I've always been there for others; now, I need to be fully present for myself.*

I wanted to explore the changes unfolding within me. This place had profoundly impacted me, and I longed to fully experience its power, not just heal and leave. So, I extended my stay for another month.

The next day, Rozi showed me a nest with the sweetest baby hummingbirds. I saw this as a message—a symbol of my fresh start and readiness to spread my wings.

For peace of mind, I consulted my pet intuitive about my dogs. They were doing well, though Baby Puppy said she knew something was up. I also arranged for a remote Akashic Records reading and healing session with Jen, a powerful healer whom I had recently come to know. She helped me release my past, including my marriage, soul contract, and even Montezuma.

During the healing, Jen said there was no more energy there for me, and that needing to be in community was keeping me from my individual path and mastery.

To address the pain manifesting in my body, Hai referred me to Natascha, a bodyworker. When we met, it was like recognizing a sister. We shared a striking physical resemblance and similar devotion to our healing work. And then there was Jack, her black lab, who captured my heart immediately. It was clear that the Caribbean coast was providing support in every form.

After nearly two months in Puerto Viejo, I had yet to spot a sloth. I was fascinated with these gentle creatures and excited to be on the Caribbean side, since they were absent from the Nicoya Peninsula.

On one of my final mornings at Villa Gaia, just before my return to Montezuma, I was enjoying coffee in my hammock chair at dawn when a sloth lumbered toward me. I was overjoyed! I excitedly called Rozi and grabbed my camera. The sloth slowly climbed the massive tree beside me. Its serene, "permasmile" expression felt like an invitation to return. What I experienced in Gaia was profound and filled me completely. I was now ready to see my dogs and be in my dream home again.

COSMIC GAME SHOW

Returning to Montezuma after two months on the Caribbean coast, filled with love and support, felt jarringly different. The joy of arriving at my house, with the dogs leaping and Baby Puppy's excited whines, was immediately overshadowed by the crushing realization: *I had to leave.*

The pain of splitting up my two babies and saying goodbye to Doggie Boy and this place crashed down on me. The pain was so intense that I crumpled onto the kitchen floor, my two babies held tight in my arms, as I grieved.

A month alone in the house gave me time, but not clarity. I was lost, unsure of where to live, and emotionally paralyzed from making any decisions. My dad's invite to stay in Syracuse while he and his wife were in Europe lingered in my thoughts.

It had been fifteen years since I set foot there, before Thailand. That house was a relic of my junior high and high school days, a place I subconsciously avoided because it held the pain of my teenage insecurities and the start of my unhealthy relationship patterns.

Returning to my dream house, altered by a new awareness, felt hollow. The magic had vanished, leaving a void where my energy used to reside. My winged friends, the birds, sensed the shift and stayed away. Even the howler monkey I photographed in the backyard seemed detached, as if confirming my painful truth: this place was no longer my home.

The Saturday organic market triggered an unexpected wave of emotion. I saw a woman, a kindred spirit who sold cultured cheese, and the sight of her opened the floodgates. I cried, the familiar setting a stark reminder of what we had shared and the painful truth of our separation.

My heart was heavy, and I retreated to my home and the comfort of my dogs, desperate to figure out my next steps. A brief consideration of staying in Montezuma quickly dissolved as the thought of shared dog ownership and the prospect of staying brought on another deep wave of grief.

> Dad: *Eli, I really think coming to Syracuse would be good for you. You need that time and space to heal. Please come, I want to see you before we leave. I miss you and love you so much.*
>
> Me: *Okay, yes, sounds good, perfect timing. I'll look at flights now. Thank you, Dad. I love you very much.*

Hai messaged me saying she and Rozi felt my energy in Puerto Viejo. "My spirit is there," I replied, "but my body is in Montezuma."

Later that day, in a Puerto Viejo WhatsApp group, I saw a message that seemed meant for me. A woman was seeking someone with deeper knowledge of candida, beyond the standard diet stuff. I was shocked; I hadn't seen that kind of question in Costa Rica or in a WhatsApp group.

I responded, sending her one of my YouTube videos, "Let me know if this resonates." She watched it instantly and signed up for my six-week class right away. It felt like another confirmation that my Spirit was in Puerto Viejo.

Before leaving for Syracuse, I scheduled a reading with Alex, my favorite psychic, to connect with my dogs about my travel plans and get some guidance about my move to Puerto Viejo upon my return.

The day before my appointment, my neighbor and friend, Coco, who also happens to be an excellent psychic and tarot reader, invited me over. As we sat on her bed, chatting about my upcoming move while she shuffled her cards, she suddenly stopped.

"Elicia," she said, "I know you don't want to hear this, but a great love is coming."

"Yeah, I really don't," I replied. "I'm craving solitude right now."

The very next day, during my scheduled reading with Alex, we discussed my decision to move to Puerto Viejo. And then she said the same thing: "Elicia, I know you don't want to hear this, but a great love is coming." Hearing those identical words two days in a row definitely made me take notice, though I put it in the back of my mind.

Leaving for Syracuse was more complicated than I expected. My emotions were running so high that I didn't realize I was a day late for my flight until I reached the check-in counter. I was devastated, and my stomach dropped as tears streamed down my face. It was Friday, and the next available flight wasn't until Monday, which would have been incredibly expensive.

Thankfully, Delta's customer service found a solution: I spent the night in San Jose, flew to Atlanta the next day, stayed in an airport hotel, and then caught an early flight to New York City and finally landed in Syracuse.

As it turned out, those extra nights and the unplanned visits with dear friends in each city were exactly what I needed to prepare for my return to my teenage home.

After two wonderful days with my dad and his wife, I finally had the house to myself. It struck me that I hadn't lived in such a spacious home in years, and the freedom to move around felt exhilarating.

I queued up a music channel on my dad's impressive TV, the sound pouring out through his audiophile speakers. Then, I lost myself in the music, dancing and singing along to REM, New Order, Violent Femmes, Bauhaus, and The Cure. Each song was a portal back to high school, but this time, I was fully present, joyful, and filled with self-love.

Driving to the nearby shopping center, a wave of nostalgia washed over me as I remembered cruising with friends in my old 1980s diesel VW Rabbit listening to N.W.A.

I walked into a thrift shop, and they were also playing all my high school favorites. I couldn't resist buying a pair of sky-blue Jordache jeans. It felt like my teenage self had returned, fully embracing who we've become.

With Sinead O'Connor's "Feel So Different" playing, the drive home became a journey of gratitude and liberation. I felt profoundly changed, as if a heavy burden had finally been lifted.

My best friend from high school, Christy, joined me at the house, and we had a night filled with champagne, laughter, and our favorite music. I was excited to talk about Sinead O'Connor's documentary, but she hadn't seen it. "Let's watch it soon," I suggested.

The following day, while relaxing in the hot tub, my phone lit up with notifications—Sinead O'Connor died. My heart ached, and tears flowed down my face into the water. So many people reached out because they knew how much her music meant to me, especially the song "Troy."

That song defined my teenage years, forever associated with an older boy I was infatuated with starting at fourteen years old. The way he used and discarded me marked the beginning of my dysfunctional patterns with men.

In my twenties, my late-night party crew knew that an a cappella rendition of "Troy" was almost guaranteed. My friends knew me so well that a simple "It was a Troy night" was all the communication we needed.

While I was staying in the same room where those feelings and patterns began, I heard this news. It felt like the universe was pulling me back to my past for one last, powerful encounter.

Going further back, my elementary school friend, Jenny, reached out. We hadn't seen each other since we lived on the same street forty years ago.

Our reunion was full of joy, and we hugged tightly. After a delicious Mexican dinner, we strolled through the park across the street, and that's when we heard the news: Paul Reubens, Pee-wee Herman, had just died. Another surreal coincidence, as we used to watch *Pee-wee's Playhouse* together.

And then, as if to confirm the saying that *things come in threes*, my mom's dog, my little "sister," died while I was in Syracuse. She was the last dog my parents had together in this house before their divorce. It felt like I was caught in some elaborate, cosmic game of "Elicia, This Is Your Life!"

To add to everything, Christy's little sister got married while I was visiting, and I was warmly included in the celebration. Seeing Christy's mom and witnessing her tears as she saw us together was incredibly moving. It was also the first time I truly enjoyed being back in Syracuse. I appreciated the new graffiti art downtown and felt surprisingly at peace and comfortable in my teenage home.

As I booked my return to Costa Rica, the Atlanta layover felt like a sign. I knew I wasn't emotionally prepared to face Montezuma: packing up my life and splitting up our dogs, and the uncertainty of when I would return to the US.

I decided to book a one-way ticket to Atlanta and stay longer with my friend Jocelyn. After picking me up from the airport, as I stepped out of her car, my jeans ripped at the seam. The sheer absurdity of it hit us both at once. We doubled over in laughter, tears streaming as Joc snapped a photo of my exposed butt cheek – a moment forever immortalized.

After settling in, we instantly fell into our flow and realized we are fantastic roommates, and, predictably, spent much of our time in fits of laughter on the floor.

The two weeks I spent in Atlanta were deeply fulfilling and truly magical. I had three beautiful photo shoots, including one with Kady, a shamanic healer who provided deep healing and clear guidance.

I rekindled a friendship, and, after nearly two decades of silence, even exchanged heartfelt messages with my first husband, Justin, who had also clearly done some deep healing and offered a sincere apology.

As a gesture of gratitude to Jocelyn for her hospitality, I took her to my favorite Tex-Mex restaurant near my beloved loft. After dinner, we wandered through Cabbagetown, admiring the vibrant street art.

Just before we entered the Krog Street tunnel, I paused at 97 Estoria, flooded with fond memories of my friend who had tragically passed away from brain cancer in 2020.

At that exact moment, a mutual friend of ours rode by on his bicycle, calling out, "Hi, Elicia!" I knew our friend above had orchestrated that little encounter. After showing Jocelyn the schoolhouse loft building where I used to live, we strolled back to her car. And then, near 97 Estoria again, I heard someone call my name. I turned to see my very first roommate in Atlanta from 1996. Okay, yes, I thought, *this is absolutely my life.*

The night before my departure, I closed my eyes, and my hands pressed gently against my heart. A wave of peace washed over me as I smiled, feeling a profound sense of closure—as if a circle, years in the making, had finally completed its turn through my past.

FEMININE FILTER

Armed with the strength Atlanta had given me, I returned to my dream home in Montezuma for the last time. Ten days alone with the dogs were dedicated to packing for my new life with Baby Puppy on the Caribbean coast. This return felt different; I was detached and focused solely on the task.

On the third day, a crisis arose: the water tank was empty, and the water supply was cut off for the weekend. The basic necessities of cleaning, washing, and drinking were suddenly unavailable.

I had to carry large water bottles from a neighbor's house. The physical strain, combined with my emotional turmoil, resulted in a complete breakdown on the patio. There was no help, no support system. Montezuma was sending a clear message: nothing was left for me here.

While I searched for a long-term rental on the Caribbean coast, Rozi offered for me to rent her other Airbnb, Villa Cefiro (meaning "gentle breeze" in Spanish).

It was a breath of fresh air after the emotionally heavy two months at Villa Gaia. Baby Puppy had a difficult time, developing separation anxiety due to the upheaval.

I started taking her everywhere with me, which benefited us both. It slowed my pace and met her deep need for social interaction. She loves being with people and the exhilarating TukTuk rides along the beach.

Our daily two-hour beach walks along the magical path to the ocean filled us both with joy. Baby Puppy needed a yard, so finding a house with a private, fenced yard became my top priority.

During my travels, Hai had been my constant lifeline; we exchanged messages daily. Now, living in the same place allowed us to enjoy deep talks over meals, meet on the beach with our girl doggies, and spend quality time with our cherished friends.

The Caribbean's energy was gentle and feminine, a refreshing change from the masculine intensity of Montezuma. I had truly arrived on the other side. My femininity and sensuality, which had felt dormant, began to blossom again.

Ending a decade-long relationship was incredibly destabilizing. A rekindled friendship in Atlanta provided support, but I likely leaned on him too heavily. The constant communication was overwhelming, and he abruptly stopped talking to me.

After feeling safe with him, his sudden silence was a shock, triggering deep sadness and anger. Two weeks into this emotional turmoil, I reached out to Sweetheart, an intuitive trauma healer and counselor, someone I had worked with before and often recommended to my clients.

During our session, she connected to my inner child's experiences, revealing a prior trauma that needed resolution. My eight-year-old self brought up a memory of repressed sexual abuse by my childhood friend's brother. I could recall the surrounding events, but not the abuse itself.

Sweetheart affirmed my inherent purity and loving nature. This cleared the way for exploring the feelings of my four-year-old, who believed I was "too much" and at fault for something.

We unearthed a significant, unconscious trauma: after my paternal grandfather's death, my dad withdrew emotionally, and I believed I was the cause.

Before that, we were best buddies. I remembered the endless playing and laughing, chasing me around the house, screaming joyfully. We shared a fun-loving connection, an emotional bond that felt unbreakable. Then, without a word, he pulled away. As a four-year-old, all I could think was, *What did I do wrong?*

This trauma had manifested repeatedly in my relationships with men, leaving me feeling that my authentic self was unacceptable. Through Sweetheart's guidance, my four-year-old self came to understand the truth: I was not responsible. My dad was simply experiencing grief and trying to shield me from it. I felt an overwhelming sense of peace and security within myself.

I now understand how this father wound activated my entire journey and how the pain and belief from that traumatic event repeatedly surfaced in all my relationships, leading to feelings of blame whenever I expressed myself fully.

Over the next six months, I went through different stages to fully return to myself.

- ~~Fantasy and obsession about a distant Bumble match.~~
- ~~Buy every online course you come across through FB ads.~~
- ~~Entertain a Latin lover idea.~~
- Be alone and happy with your dog in nature.

I moved into a magnificent "Goddess Palace" with tall vaulted ceilings, a large patio with sheer white curtains that danced in the breeze, and more space than I ever had by myself. I moved through the rooms with a lightness I hadn't felt before, finally allowing my energy to be as big as needed.

Natascha, my new friend, lived up the street with her dog, Jack. Each morning, we strolled to the beach together. Jack became River's prince, digging cool holes in the sand for her to rest in, and we formed a warm little family.

I also loved meeting up with Toni, another new friend, and his exuberant pack of four dogs. The four of us, Natascha, Toni, and Hai, would gather for pizza, play Rummikub, and share deep, supportive conversations that nourished our souls.

The week after I moved into my new Goddess Palace, a rare full solar eclipse took place in Puerto Viejo, the only location in Costa Rica where it could be seen in its entirety. People across the country had planned this trip for years. It felt like total serendipity that I happened to be there, having just arrived.

Natascha and I, along with our dogs, headed to the beach with my tripod, camera, and zoom lens. I was so excited to do a photo shoot with the solar eclipse—a once-in-a-lifetime event.

After setting up my tripod and looking through my lens, I felt sad. I quickly discovered I needed a special solar lens filter to photograph the eclipse's annular ring.

Seeing my disappointment, a kind man next to me offered me an extra filter he had, saving the day. Deeply touched, I sensed my guardian angels, another sign of the deep support here.

The solar filter worked its magic, and through my lens, I witnessed the perfect, golden half-ring of the eclipse. Pure joy radiated through me. This wasn't just any photo shoot; the eclipse's energy felt personal and powerful.

Just as the ring was about to complete, a young boy approached, his eyes wide with wonder, asking to see. His excitement reflected the child within me.

In an incredibly moving moment, the kind man who had lent me the filter knelt and proposed to his girlfriend as the full solar eclipse shone above.

An overwhelming wave of love embraced me. The resulting photos, capturing each stage of the eclipse, were breathtaking. Seeing them all together inspired me to create some truly unique collages.

Once I finished creating, I snuggled up with Baby Puppy and put on *The Crowded Room*. Amanda Seyfried's line, "Carl Jung thought eclipses were harbingers of rebirth," made me pause and take a screenshot.

The following week, my creative goddess tattoo came to life. Now, without the expansive ocean view, the moon rise, the vibrant sunrises, or the dance of birds, my creative energy shifted inward.

I began a deep process of understanding who I am, separate from my marriage and the magical "Disney Movie" setting. The photos I captured became mirrors of my soul, revealing my essence, my authentic expressions, and my deepest passions. Parts of myself that had long been hidden were revealed, finally witnessed and cherished, by my eyes and heart.

From this transformative experience, I created the True Essence Program, a playful and feminine exploration of self. The program cultivates intuition and imagery, using photography as a window to the soul, reflecting the true self. This process awakens self-awareness, nurtures self-love, and illuminates the authentic self and vision.

My inner child, Eli, gave a resounding "YES" to this new program. We knew we had completed our journey with Core Emotional Healing and returned to our inner joy. It reminded me of when I was four, bursting through the door after preschool with excitement, and eagerly asking, "Wanna see my pictures?"

Memories flooded back to me. Around that same age, I suddenly started telling myself and everyone I knew that I wasn't creative, and I even skipped art and music classes in school.

In my 20s, I surrounded myself with artists and musicians, saying, "I'm not creative, that's why I hang out with them," despite spontaneously making up silly rap songs when we were drinking.

I really believed I wasn't creative until after I completed the four years of experiential courses when I was 34—it must have originated from some early criticism of my pictures.

Then, at 45, when I first arrived in Montezuma, it finally clicked, and I knew I was an essence photographer. I burst out laughing and said, "Eli, you're a Creative Goddess and I love your pictures!"

She then whispered to me, "Now you remember." When I was three, my wise, silly girl would say, "Are you a member of the member club?" for the word "remember." Yes, I am a member, I do remember.

In an astrology and soul reading, Hugo described my energy as powerfully transformative, stating that its impact was "triple" in terms of action. He said my energy is about believing in the invisible. Each person's journey and miracle are unique.

Their intentions expand when connecting to my energy, making the impossible possible. He confirmed that I guide people toward self-love, am the mother of many, and inspire them to dream and become their true selves.

Hugo's validation of my true self and the creative and transformational process in the True Essence Program filled my inner child with boundless energy. I could see my joy mirrored in Baby Puppy's playful spirit.

Each morning, Baby Puppy visited our neighbors, spreading her love and soaking up all the social interaction and affection she thrived on. Then, in the late afternoon, I'd take her to our favorite spot, Gigi Beach Club. There, I could indulge in a bit of beachside glamour on a luxurious bed with relaxing deep house music vibrating through my body.

I savored sushi and sipped a margarita as Baby Puppy made her rounds, charming every table in search of treats and cuddles. Our new Caribbean life's easygoing, peaceful, and feminine energy was exactly what our souls craved.

My first visitors were friends from Montezuma who had been living in San Jose. Suzie and François brought their dog Castor, one of my "lover boy" labs. One evening at my palace, while playing music and dancing, I held Castor's paws and playfully sang "Shaking the Dog" to the tune of "Shaking the Tree."

My spiritual healer and friend, Rebecca, was my next visitor and finally met River. She was the one who predicted she would choose me to be her mom. We enjoyed the beach and lounging at Gigi. I did an essence photo shoot for her, and she gave me a few powerful healing sessions, helping me shed the weight and attachments from my marriage.

Before leaving, Rebecca casually mentioned a man at our usual breakfast spot, whom she thought I might find interesting.

The next time I went, I saw him, and he asked for my number. Immediately, I sensed his strong spiritual energy. Over lunch, he shared how he helps people through divine messages.

On my walk home, I spotted two sloths—my first since moving there. It felt like nature was responding to our interaction. He left the decision of seeing him again entirely up to me. I was struck by this; I hadn't encountered a man so free of pressure or expectations. He held such vastness within him, and our energetic exchange ignited a powerful activation, honoring my feminine. His aura seemed to embrace the divine feminine within me, like a mystical god holding the cosmos and the divine plan. I chose not to pursue anything further and communicated that to him. I felt deeply grateful for the experience and was fundamentally changed.

The next day, my dad called. He wanted to share a recent experience at a restaurant where he observed a little girl. Her parents were engaged in their own conversation, but she was captivating everyone around her with her joyful energy and vibrant spirit. He told me she reminded him so much of me when I was young.

Then, in a moment of vulnerability, he told me how deeply he regretted missing out on being truly present during my childhood. My eyes filled with tears of love.

After our call, I put my hand on my heart and reassured my inner child: *You are so loved and special. Dad has always seen and loved all of you, but had trouble connecting and expressing himself.*

I felt an overwhelming wave of emotion and knew, with absolute clarity, that this moment signified the healing of my father wound. It happened between my birthday and Christmas, and it felt like the most meaningful present I could have been given.

Shortly after, my friend Suzie in San Jose called to say they were coming to visit again in early February and bringing a friend, Olivier, who was flying in from France. *I wonder who he is?*

DROPS OF GOD

My time at the Goddess Palace was cut short when the owners returned. Finding another place to rent was extremely challenging because it was the high season.

During my house search, I told myself: *I am outgrowing Costa Rica.* I ended up in a temporary cabin up the street at the end of January. It was near everything I loved and tucked away in the wild jungle. That's also when I got hooked on the Apple TV+ show *Drops of God*, a fascinating French-American-Japanese drama. I felt a longing when I watched it.

Camille Léger is the estranged daughter of a renowned oenologist. She is initially disconnected from the world of wine and struggles with emotional vulnerabilities. She is thrust into a competition with her father's protégé to inherit his vast wine collection. This competition challenges her senses, knowledge, and personal growth. Throughout the series, Camille discovers her own hidden talents and passion for wine. She also confronts her past and develops a deeper understanding of her father.

I was captivated by the show's creative direction, and as a red wine enthusiast, I found myself increasingly drawn to French culture. In the evenings, I enjoyed making sheep cheese and date plates, paired with a glass of red wine. A sense of frustration began to build within me regarding the limitations in the quality of wine, organic food, housing, and infrastructure in Costa Rica.

Just days before my friends arrived with their mysterious French companion, Olivier, I settled into the cabin. I played one of those silly Facebook games, and the result predicted "a BIG surprise" for me for Valentine's Day.

Suzie, François, and Olivier were on their way from San Jose. I took River for a walk to Sushi Wave restaurant on the beach, my second favorite spot, to meet them.

When they stepped out of the car, I was immediately captivated by Olivier—I hadn't anticipated a tall man with such a gentle aura. A silver fox with crystal clear blue eyes, and a physique reminiscent of a Greek god.

The prophecy from Coco and Alex flashed through my mind: *Elicia, I know you don't want to hear this, but a great love is coming. Could it be him?*

Almost immediately, I sensed a telepathic connection between us. I felt Olivier's strong, steady presence and careful attention to detail.

At dinner, surrounded by friends, he sat diagonally from me. When I ordered the house red—typically a cabernet—they brought merlot. *Yuck.*

Olivier caught my reaction, and without a word, he went to the bar and brought back a good bottle of cabernet. I was touched by his thoughtfulness and drawn to his energy. He remained composed, making no advances, which was a refreshing change. I later discovered he had journeyed from France to meet me, which was a tremendous risk, so he waited for me to show interest.

Outside, as we waited for the car, I felt his gaze and sensed he was holding back. I turned to him and asked, "So, do you want to kiss?" The kiss, that lasted all night, sensual and tender, with the sweetest lips, was unlike anything I had ever felt. My heart knew he was my great love.

Olivier's presence filled me with such vibrant energy that I couldn't sleep. The feel of his skin was electric. Baby Puppy also fell instantly in love with him.

Olivier gifted me a high-quality olive oil and Lancome Zen face lotion with rose, which were thoughtful presents he brought for me from France. I felt love in my heart as I smelled the rose lotion. The three of us strolled to the beach to join Suzie and François at my favorite breakfast café, and it was clear to everyone that we were a perfect match.

I immediately recognized Olivier as my spiritual match, just as he did when he first saw a video and then a photo of me. After a week together, he shared the story behind his arrival.

A few months prior, François had recorded a video of me dancing to "Shaking the Tree" and playfully singing to his dog, "Shaking the Dog." This video reached Olivier in December, and his instant reaction was, "Who is that beautiful woman?"

François thought I wouldn't be interested and that it might be too soon after my separation, so he initially discouraged him. The following month, he spontaneously sent Olivier a wedding photo of himself and Suzie, where I was beaming in it.

Olivier said my smile pierced his heart, and he fell in love with me right then. His heart and soul recognized me, and following his intuition, he booked a flight right away to come meet me, without me knowing.

Olivier spent a month preparing to meet me by brushing up on his English and envisioning our first encounter. It was a real-life French romance fairytale.

Within the first week, it was clear we were in love and meant to be together. Olivier immediately changed his flight to extend his stay by a month, wanting to spend as much time with me as possible before returning to France for his next film.

For most of his career, Olivier had been a key grip, responsible for the intricate work of setting up and maintaining all the camera equipment, ensuring everything was secure and safe from falls.

Just before Valentine's Day, we had pedicures done by a man who was set to play Cupid in a drag show. It was only the day after Valentine's that I finally noticed a Cupid decoration hanging on my cabin door that had been there all along. I moved into this place just three days before Olivier's arrival.

In Roman mythology, Cupid—the son of Mercury, messenger of the gods, and Venus, the goddess of love—is depicted as a winged infant armed with a bow and quiver, whose arrows spark love in those they strike. And it seemed I was destined to be struck.

Over the next month, Olivier met me fully, embracing my vulnerability. My "too much" was just right for him and he loved it. I always felt deeply cared for. The joy I expressed through silly songs was mirrored by his own—he'd play the drums with his fingers on the counter to my song and dance while making breakfast. We both danced freely throughout the day. He anticipated our every need, taking care of things before I needed to ask. He cooked, cleaned, did laundry, and thoughtfully stocked the kitchen.

Olivier's humor was also a constant source of joy. He would call out "My Sirena!"—Spanish for mermaid—when I approached the water, waving his arms dramatically.

Each day, the three of us—Baby Puppy included—would stroll along the shore to Gigi Beach Club, where we ordered a refreshing margarita for me and a cool, minty mojito for Olivier. We would then spend hours laughing and lounging on the beach bed.

Our creative sides also meshed beautifully. He expressed himself through stunning drone videos with musical scores, while I created my own musical narratives with photos and videos.

While we were relaxing on Gigi's beach bed, I received messages from my ex. Instantly, I was pulled back into the vortex of our painful interactions. A wave of grief washed over me, tears streaming down my face.

Olivier gathered me into his strong arms, his embrace warm and comforting. "It's okay," he murmured softly. "Shhh, I'm here now. You don't need to worry anymore."

I experienced a depth of comfort and care in Olivier's arms I'd never known. He listened to my heart and embraced my vulnerability completely. It was the first time I felt truly held, not just physically, but in spirit—a love that didn't ask me to change, just to be. I realized then that this was a love unlike any I had experienced before: Olivier, my sensitive King.

It's incredible to think that our paths crossed four times in the same cities over the last thirty-six years, yet we never met. Olivier visited New York twice while I was there, and I went to Paris on my first international trip while he lived there.

He even went to Montezuma almost yearly for fifteen years, ending his visits just before I moved there. It was as if our souls had been searching for each other since the beginning of time.

I had thought I never wanted to live with anyone again, feeling utterly drained in past relationships. Olivier felt the same and had remained single for twenty years.

But with each other, it was completely different. We were energized, perfectly attuned in our loving care, detail, and empathy. Our affection was tender and sweet, and our chemistry sparked.

A beautiful dance between two loving, positive, adventurous fire signs. *Oh, the profound joy of living with my perfect match. Finally, my reward.*

To awaken each morning to "Bonjour, my love" and a tender kiss, followed by a gentle "How did you sleep?" was a healing balm for my heart.

As Olivier's time with me drew to a close, my new friend and client, Harmony, the one who posted on the WhatsApp group about candida, invited us to her fiancé's birthday party on the beach.

It was wonderful to finally meet Harmony in person. Her fiancé, Vlad, who spoke fluent French, had a conversation with Olivier. Afterward, we enjoyed a stroll hand-in-hand along the beach. Olivier filmed a beautiful drone video of us, capturing the scene as I sat nestled between his legs in the sand, and panning out to the sparkling ocean stretching beyond Cocles Island.

During his last days with me in Puerto Viejo, I would look at him, and tears would flood my eyes, thinking about him leaving. Olivier said, "Don't think about it, let's enjoy every moment together. I can fly back whenever you want."

At our last lunch at Grow, we sat next to Hannah. She'd only known me as a single woman, so seeing me with Olivier, so obviously happy and in love, gave her pause. Our discussion about a potential trade—an essence photo shoot for her, and a shamanic journey for me—felt especially significant.

As Olivier's departure approached, he showed me a vertical hummingbird nest, a miniature miracle attached to a leaf next to my porch. It was a beautiful, tender moment we shared right before the sadness of saying goodbye.

I was deeply curious about the hummingbird babies, wondering if I would witness their hatching, growth, and ultimately, their first flight. I knew there was only a thirty percent chance they would survive this delicate stage.

After Olivier left, sleep was impossible. Nights were filled with tossing and turning, but in our dreams, we were reunited. We would wake up in the dark, reaching for each other, only to find emptiness and feel sad.

Suddenly, my beach life felt empty. I walked around lost, constantly asking myself, *What am I doing here? I don't feel at home anymore.*

Five sleepless nights later, at two in the morning, Olivier's friend's question came back to me: "Why doesn't Elicia just move to France?" *Why not?* I already longed for French wine, cheese, and that undeniable quality in everything.

I knew then that I was ready to leave Costa Rica and everything it represented behind—my engagement to Marc twenty years prior, the thirty-day water fast, and my ex and our life.

I was ready to close my Costa Rica chapter, with all its highs and lows, and embrace a new life in France with Olivier. Costa Rica had been my cocoon, both sanctuary and struggle, but now I was ready for more. Björk's "There's More to Life Than This" pulsed through me, a visceral confirmation for my yearning for something more.

I shared my decision to move to France with Olivier; his reaction was pure joy. A wave of relief washed over us both. And for the first time in days, we both slept soundly, filled with dreams of our future together.

The most daunting challenge, undoubtedly, was orchestrating the move for both Baby Puppy and me. It was a complex undertaking that required a significant amount of logistical planning and emotional support.

ECLIPSE PORTAL

I dreamt of photographing hummingbird eggs from a ladder, which prompted me to stand on a chair on my porch the next day. I extended my camera with my longest zoom lens overhead and took a photo to check on the nest without disturbing the eggs or the mama.

I was greeted by an even more wonderful sight: tiny, newly hatched babies. Seeing them was incredibly touching, and I quickly grew attached to them. Over the next week, on my porch, the mama hummingbird hovered anxiously around me, seemingly stressed as she tried to feed her young. I worried there might not be enough food for them.

Around that time, I did a shamanic journey with Hannah. My intention was to release my old life and move forward into my new one. Hannah works with the spirit of Ayahuasca, without needing the physical medicine.

There was so much French influence that day. Although Hannah is Welsh, she was born in Paris and lived there as a young child. Her husband had a friend visiting them from France, and he even shared the same name as Olivier's middle name.

During the journey, I released my attachments to my ex and Costa Rica, my inner child was overjoyed with love thinking about Olivier, and I had a powerful vision: I stood among priestesses in France, receiving gifts from above.

That evening, I wanted to watch something easy and fun, so I watched a movie that was just released on Apple TV+ called *Argylle*. As the story unfolded, I was floored by the parallels with what was happening in my life.

It's about a writer whose love takes her from the US to the South of France, to remember who she really is. Olivier called Baby Puppy "The Keeper," and while the main character is in the South of France, they go to see a woman they call "The Keeper." It was a lot to take in, so I paused the movie.

I closed my eyes, and a memory resurfaced of the shamanic journey from twelve years prior, after my miscarriage with Nic. During that experience, the shaman woman told me that once I stopped "trying to make him understand," I would reunite with a part of myself waiting for me on a balcony in the South of France, laughing her ass off enjoying wine. This prediction suddenly made sense and blew my mind. I had assumed it was metaphorical, not literal.

When I told my friend Anna, who creates flower essences, about my move, she reminded me of Mary Magdalene's nearby cave. She shared a photo of the cover of a Mary Magdalene book she was reading, the same book Hannah had shown me that same day. This made me wonder if Mary was a guiding force, connecting me with Olivier.

Following the journey with Hannah, I experienced intense abdominal pain. Just as I focused on my body to find relief, a local bodyworker specializing in emotional release posted on WhatsApp. This led to a more intense three-hour journey involving physical-emotional release, including screaming and grieving, to finally let go of deeply held pain. The pain left, and I felt lighter.

After the emotional release, I arrived home and felt the absence of the mama hummingbird. I used my zoom lens to look into the nest to confirm my uneasy feeling. I saw two tiny hollow skeletons, dry, brown, and decaying.

While grieving the loss, I recognized the symbolism—this represented the lingering energy of my ex and solidified the ending of our union and all that we went through. I put my hand on my heart and quietly said, *Thank you.*

For the fourth time, I found myself releasing most of my belongings. My electric scooter, JBL Boombox, and aerial silks went up for sale on a local Buy/Sell WhatsApp group, and everything else was lovingly given to my dear friends Hai, Natascha, and Toni.

This process felt familiar; I'd done the same before moving to Thailand. I deeply value that my friends hold onto these pieces of me as reminders of our enduring bonds.

I faced the challenge of handling the one-year extended French visa application entirely on my own.

Since it required application in the US, River and I had to travel there first.

Juggling flight schedules, River's health certificates from the vets in both Costa Rica and the US, and the uncertainty of the visa timeline was incredibly overwhelming. I maintained faith and focused on each step, believing everything would ultimately align.

As our final beach walk with Natascha and Jack drew to a close, River bounded back and forth with Jack, a very fitting "Baby Puppy" send-off. Natascha and I both cried.

The next night, I shared a special dinner with Hai at a restaurant we both had been wanting to try—a little more upscale than our usual spots. We cherished our connection and support over the past year, celebrating our many changes. Then, on my last night in the Caribbean, Hai, Natascha, and Toni gathered for pizza and our final, tender goodbyes.

As the shuttle doors closed, carrying my two suitcases and River, I felt like I was entering a portal, shutting the Costa Rica chapter to leap into the unknown. I signed my divorce papers in San Jose on the day of the solar eclipse, April 8th, during a powerful eclipse season. It truly felt like a *total eclipse of my heart*.

Back in Atlanta, staying with Jocelyn, I faced the complex French visa application. The shift from the vibrant jungle to a city condo shocked us both. River trembled from the cold and the unfamiliar surroundings, while I battled daily with what felt like an impending nervous breakdown.

Adding to my anxiety, I realized my passport was expiring in a year and needed immediate renewal. Luckily, I had already booked my flight to France, so I could secure a same-day renewal.

Waiting in the downtown office, my turn came. The woman who called me had a name plate that read "Gigi," the same name as our favorite beach club in Costa Rica. That very week, on the series "Emily in Paris," Gabriel named his dream restaurant "Gigi." Shining light and sprinkling levity onto the stress, life continued to offer support and reassurance.

I hired a visa assistance service, but their slow responses prolonged the process and amplified my stress. "Visa delay service" would have been a more accurate name. I was consumed with fear and doubt each day, waiting for their replies to my documents and questions.

What if I don't get an appointment for another month?

Where will I live? I can't get a place until I know how long I will need to be here.

What if I don't get a visa?

I have no home, no car, and nowhere else I want to go.

I am away from my love.

River needs a yard; we need a house.

Throughout the two months we were apart, Olivier showered me with affection. Every day, I received photos of him sending kisses, accompanied by messages like "Bonjour mon amour" and rows of heart, dog, love, and kiss emojis. His videos were filled with sweet expressions of love and unwavering support.

Meanwhile, he transformed his house into our home, meticulously cleaning and organizing. He stocked up on River's special dog food, prepared a room for my office, and cleaned out the closet for all my things. Our love and anticipation for our reunion kept us connected as we each worked toward creating our shared future.

The day I had to renew my passport, my mom arrived, and her presence was a true godsend. I picked her up at the airport with River, and we enjoyed Thai food before picking up my new passport.

In the same condo complex as Jocelyn lived another dear friend, Jody, a truly gifted healer. All three of us had been connected years before Jocelyn moved there. Jody also offered me invaluable support during this period. I was fortunate to experience her signature spinal release therapy, which brought about the most profound relaxation.

During a walk with River, I shared the anxieties of my transition with Jody. We then drove to the Publix supermarket so I could grab some chocolate. The woman in front of me was wearing sandals with the word "Paris" embroidered on the strap. Synchronistic signs of reassurance were appearing at every turn.

Near the end of the month, I secured a visa appointment in Miami. River and I drove to my aunt's home in

South Florida to rest and recharge. It was a special time connecting with my aunt. Coincidentally, my cousin and his fiancé were also visiting for the weekend before their wedding.

Olivier flew in from France to join us. He came to help me until my visa was issued so we could embark on our journey to France together as a family.

I was buzzing with excitement to meet Olivier at the airport, so much so that River and I arrived two hours ahead of schedule. It gave me time to find the ideal spot for our first moments together—a place to eat, have a drink, and share those longed-for kisses. I chose the restaurant across from his gate and ordered our meal, taking a moment to calm my butterflies. "There he is," I said softly to River as he emerged.

Our embrace was like something out of a dream, a surreal culmination of our journey so far. Our initial plan was for this reunion to be in Paris, but fate had brought us to South Florida, still on the brink of our new life.

River's tail thumped with joy, but it was the sound of Olivier's familiar voice when it all clicked. "Oh! It's you, Papa!" she cried out with her Baby Puppy excited whining as she jumped up on his legs for kisses. In that embrace, it felt like we had finally found our home.

The visa delay, while initially frustrating, was an unexpected gift. It allowed me to introduce Olivier to the people and places I hold dear before we embarked on our life in France.

I booked an Airbnb in my favorite Atlanta neighborhood, Inman Park, for us and my dad, who flew in from Syracuse to meet Olivier and say goodbye. I was thrilled to show Olivier my loft and Little 5 Points. We spent wonderful days with my dad walking and enjoying Inman Park's restaurants with River. My heart overflowed with gratitude for my friend's and family's support, and their blessings as we embarked on our journey to France.

THE SCENT OF ROSES

Our arrival in France fell on Mother's Day and coincided with Olivier's work in Saintes-Maries-de-la-Mer. While he worked, I played with River on the beach. Even though I wasn't fully recovered from the trip, the energy there was invigorating and lifted me up.

Exploring the village, I passed quaint shops and came upon a shrine. There, I learned that this very shore was where Mary Magdalene first sought refuge in France, fleeing persecution in Palestine. Chills ran through my body and up to my head—we had both arrived in the *same* place.

I felt as if Mary was walking beside me. I heard a voice within me say, "I am so happy you are here. You are exactly where you need to be." I sighed deeply as I felt a wave of relief wash over me.

We drove through the breathtaking lavender fields of Provence, close to our house on the organic farm. When we arrived, I got out of the car, and River burst forth, running joyfully around the farm. She knew she was home. Seeing her so happy was even more confirmation. Not just a yard, but an entire farm to explore; it was perfect for her.

Olivier's half-sister, Claire, and her partner, who owns the farm, came to welcome us with their two border collies. I paused, awestruck, as the reality of it all sank in. *I had done it.* After two months of nonstop stress and hurdles, we were here, starting a life together on this idyllic farm in the South of France.

Next to our home were rows of white tunnel greenhouses growing organic produce. I thought, *You can't get more local and seasonal than this. This is the quality of life I have been craving.*

The sight of the clothesline and Tibetan prayer flags fluttering in the wind brought a sense of peace. A red rose bush by the door felt like Mary Magdalene's personal greeting.

Sitting on the porch, admiring the olive tree Olivier had planted for us, he offered me the juiciest, sweetest strawberries I had ever tasted. Then, with a smile, Olivier uncorked the champagne he bought to celebrate our new life together, and we raised a toast, "À ta santé!"

I had a dream about the Holy Spirit that week that stayed with me. In the dream, I felt the Holy Spirit's pure love energy and the contrast between that and human empathy.

When I woke up, I walked River down the driveway and was suddenly surrounded by the scent of roses. I looked down and found a small dried bouquet of roses on the ground right at my feet. I held the bouquet and took a photo, feeling the tangible presence of the Holy

Spirit and Mary Magdalene. This experience helped me feel more connected, as I was still searching for my footing in this new, strange land.

Creating our new home together was fun and easy. We shopped for River's new French bed, leash, and collar. My office quickly took shape, and I was thrilled to discover that my closet held all my belongings perfectly, even shelves ideal for my camera and lenses.

To personalize my workspace, I ordered a desk and had two of my favorite photos printed on canvas: a contented sloth in a Caribbean jungle tree with vines, and one with three starfish in the turquoise sea I took during a quick trip to Bocas del Toro, Panama.

Bathed in light, my office was a bright and cheerful space that instantly lifted my spirits. The fig tree outside my window inspired my creativity, as figs resemble a mother's womb.

The transition from Costa Rica's vibrant, lush jungle to the South of France's stark, open countryside was a significant adjustment, and it took months before I truly felt grounded and connected to the land.

I was drawn to the farm's abundant sunflowers, a vibrant tapestry of reds, yellows, and oranges, and I absorbed their positive, bright energy. There was something magical about photographing the bees; their dance among the heart of the tiny blossoms felt like a secret, beautiful world.

At first, the organic Saturday market at our doorstep felt daunting due to the language barrier. Thankfully, Olivier guided me through the local vendors: fresh, creamy goat cheese and yogurt, an array of the best bread in the world, aromatic organic coffee and teas, homemade quiches and pies, oyster mushrooms from a nearby farm, local honey, and of course, the produce was grown where we lived. Saturday quickly became River's favorite day; she thrived on the social interaction and spent most of her time contentedly by the butcher's side.

My social interaction was limited to the Saturday market and short conversations with Claire on the farm. When Olivier began a two-month job with long hours, I felt isolated and missed the entertainment of my previous life. I explored with River, but found more comfort at home. It was a peaceful, comfortable, modern sanctuary, and I embraced a new, more solitary flow.

It dawned on me that my new life, stripped of all distractions and entertainment, was exactly what I needed to write my book—a personal writer's retreat. Olivier's workday and my client calls, now in the late afternoon, gifted me hours of solitude.

The farm's tranquility allowed me to rest, delve deep within, and unlock a wellspring of memories. I was present in a way I had never been. The ten hours a day of silence allowed my memoir to finally flow.

I began to truly appreciate French culture and their emphasis on leisure and months of vacation. In the summer, we drove to Spain and spent two weeks on the beach with Olivier's family, and Baby Puppy expressed her boundless joy.

By the time fall rolled around, just as I was craving social connection and fun, a few friends from different countries happened to be visiting nearby. We met a couple I knew from Costa Rica for a fancy lunch in Marseille. Then, Ange, my best friend from San Francisco, came to Paris with her husband, so Olivier, River, and I hopped on the TGV for a quick overnight trip. Spending time with my "creative goddess tattoo" soul sister, Ange, infused me with love and joy.

Our life together on the farm was filled with pure sweetness and fun-loving happiness. River bonded with Claire's dog, Pitou, and Claire became a loving presence in her life. Olivier took wonderful care of us and always listened attentively to me.

Our kitchen became a stage for a lighthearted musical, with silly songs, dancing, and laughter. As I sat on the balcony, sipping Côte-Rôtie and laughing my ass off, I merged into the very prophecy the shaman had foretold.

Only an hour away from our house is the sacred sanctuary of Sainte-Baume, the cave where Mary Magdalene is said to have spent her last thirty years in quiet contemplation. The hike up to the cave was mystical. As sunlight filtered through the ancient forest, every step felt like a pilgrimage. In the main cave where they hold services, water dripped down from the ceiling, and I felt a sense of peace and serenity wash over me.

I placed a flickering candle before one of Mary's statues. Tears streamed down my face, overtaken by a feeling beyond the boundaries of my conscious mind. With each step down the stairs, I descended deeper within myself. I saved the tricky hike to the Cave of Eggs for another day.

A month later, prepared with rope and a carabiner, I trekked to Mary's Cave of Eggs. The sight was awe-inspiring—a sacred natural wonder, the tall mountain folds looked exactly like the yoni of the Goddess.

Descending into the cave felt like entering my womb. Chills ran through me, followed by absolute silence. Everywhere, small, medium, and large yoni caves opened up. My gaze was drawn to another cave below, and I sat mesmerized by a natural flower shape in the rock. I slipped into meditation, feeling Mary's presence and healing energy wash over me.

Alone in her cave, now in my cave, I felt her message: *You've come so far, sister. I walked this path too. Your past and pain are gone; this is a new beginning. Live from this higher place.*

The remaining heaviness and worries from my past lifted, and I emerged from Mary Magdalene's Cave of Eggs feeling reborn.

EPILOGUE

I'm sitting on my porch with my completed manuscript on my lap. I breathe deeply, inhaling the scent of roses, and smile at Baby Puppy rolling in the grass. Two doves land on the tree in front of me, and in this moment, I feel what I have been seeking all along—true peace and love.

Now that I am 50 years old, I embrace my short hair, fair skin, small bust, and menopausal body with a newfound sense of freedom, beauty, and confidence. It's funny. I used to say in my twenties, "I can't wait until I'm 50." Now, I truly understand the wisdom in that insight.

I gently place my hands on my heart and tell my inner child and teenager, "You were always perfect, just as you were: beautiful, wild, funny, brave, sweet, and inspiring. You've always been the leader."

I've learned to listen to my feelings, stand firm against abuse and mistreatment, and be guided by wisdom, clarity, and strength. I never give up, holding a loving space for others to achieve what seems impossible—a true gift of transformation.

I embrace expressing my feelings and playful humor authentically whenever and however I desire, with love and joy pouring through.

Reflecting on my journey, I realize we must walk this path ourselves, yet we are never truly alone. Healing into wholeness demands the dedication of a heart warrior, unwavering faith, patience, deep listening, and the invaluable support of our earth angels.

Life always holds more to unfold, but for now, I am at home within myself. At that moment, a dove fluttered its wings, and I felt the sacred in everything.

ACKNOWLEDGMENTS

I'm deeply thankful to my inner child and body for being so strong, wise, and patient throughout my journey to reconnect with you.

To my mom and dad, thank you for raising me the best that you could and allowing me to find my own path. I'm so grateful we've been able to heal and build such a close and supportive relationship.

To Hudson, Molly, Brocco, Girl, and River (my sweet baby puppy!), my furry companions and teachers, thank you for your unwavering love.

To Olivier, my Great Love, I am so grateful that you listened to your heart and came to Costa Rica to find me. Thank you for loving me and Baby Puppy so completely. You are my sweet, funny, sensitive King.

And for my psychics, Alex and Coco, thank you for giving me the heads up about my Great Love. Thank you, Suzie and François, for bringing him to me.

To my relationship mirrors, and especially to you, Doug, thank you for your part in my healing and the realization of my gifts.

I'm so thankful for all my healers, teachers, earth angels, and deep friendships. Especially to Eva Andrea, my book angel; Harmony, my fairy godmother cheerleader; Hai, my lifeline; and Holly, my fellow pattern seer. You were there for me every step of the way during my rebirth and the birth of this book.

Hugo, I'm especially grateful for your astrology and channeling gifts and for bringing my book angel, Eva Andrea, into my life.

I'm grateful for the messages of support and confirmation I receive from the animals and birds.

Thank you for this quiet house on the farm in the South of France, my writer's retreat, where I was held fast until my book was birthed into the world.

To Rebecca Slaven, my constant spiritual support for the past seven years and more. Your guidance and healing have been instrumental in my journey, and I am thrilled to experience all of the visions you held close to your heart coming true.

I want to acknowledge and thank Shanda and Mary at Transcendent Publishing for their invaluable work on my book.

Thank you, Mary Magdalene.

ABOUT THE AUTHOR

If you met Elicia Woodford in a beach restaurant on the Mediterranean Sea, you'd first notice her sparkling blue-green eyes—deep, knowing, as if she had lived a hundred lives in this one. She'd greet you with warmth and effortless elegance, and within moments, you'd sense the fire of someone who has walked through love and loss, and death and rebirth four times over and emerged with a story to tell.

She would lean in, speaking with the quiet intensity of someone who has unearthed truth not only for herself, but also for others.

"Healing," she'd say, "isn't about fixing what's broken—it's about reclaiming what was always whole."

As the founder of Core Emotional Healing®, she has spent two decades guiding others to release their layers of pain and rediscover their light.

Her book, *Free To Be Me*, is a memoir that doesn't shy away from the depths. It is raw and soul-gripping—a journey through the fire of love, suffering, and the profound beauty of emotional healing.

She wrote it not just to tell her story but to offer a mirror for those longing to break free from symptoms and find love in its truest, most transformative form.

And just as the espresso cools in front of her, she'd smile, almost as if sharing a secret.

"When I'm not writing or supporting others, you'll find me wandering through lavender fields, beaches, and vineyards, camera in hand, my dog River and my Great Love by my side, gathering moments like treasures. Because healing," she'd say, "isn't just a destination—it's in the way we live, love, and see the world."

BONUS GIFT

Sign up for your free gift "Connect To Your Inner Guidance System" on my website:

eliciawoodford.com/book-gift

A guide to strengthen your connection to your inner guidance.

Includes journaling questions to:

- Strengthen your intuition.
- Make decisions with confidence.
- Connect with your emotions in a deep, healing way.

The worksheet provides specific journaling prompts for self-care and creating a life you love.

It also includes questions to ask yourself when receiving advice from others or dealing with inner criticism.

Embark on a journey of self-discovery. By answering the questions in the worksheet, you will open a doorway to deeper connection with your authentic feelings, intuition, and inner compass—guiding you toward more inner peace and joy.

For further exploration, you'll also find a directory of valuable links to the healers and retreats featured in this memoir.

Created by Elicia Woodford, Founder of Core Emotional Healing®

www.ingramcontent.com/pod-product-compliance
Lightning Source LLC
LaVergne TN
LVHW022233080526
838199LV00123B/622/J